Managerial and Technical Motivation

Assessing Needs for Achievement, Power and Affiliation

Michael J. Stahl

PRAEGER SPECIAL STUDIES • PRAEGER SCIENTIFIC

New York • Westport, Connecticut • London

Library of Congress Cataloging-in-Publication Data

Stahl, Michael J.
  Managerial and technical motivation.

  "Praeger special studies. Praeger scientific."
  Bibliography: p.
  Includes index.
  1. Employee motivation   I. Title.
HF5549.5.M63S67   1986   658.3'14   86-3221
ISBN 0-275-92068-2 (alk. paper)

Library of Congress Catalog Card Number: 86-3221
ISBN: 0-275-92068-2

First published in 1986

Praeger Publishers, 521 Fifth Avenue, New York, NY 10175
A division of Greenwood Press, Inc.

Printed in the United States of America

The paper used in this book complies with the Permanent
Paper Standard issued by the National Information Standards
Organization (Z39.48-1984).

10 9 8 7 6 5 4 3 2 1

Preface

Many intellectual debts associated with this book need to be acknowledged.

David McClelland, currently of Harvard University, has extensively described the theory concerning needs for achievement, affiliation, and power over time in such a way as to capture the fascination of countless researchers interested in motivation within organizational settings. This book could not have been written without his theoretical contributions. Indeed, this book starts with his theory and develops an innovative method to measure power, achievement, and affiliation. The research focuses on adults in organizational contexts, with particular emphasis on managers and technical professionals.

Joseph Steger, currently president of the University of Cincinnati, stimulated my thinking on managerial motivation when I conducted my doctoral studies under his direction at Rensselaer Polytechnic Institute in the early 1970s. Steger's (1978) research on the identification of managerial talent indicated that need for power is one of the most potent characteristics discriminating between effective and noneffective managers.

Adrian Harrell, currently of the University of South Carolina, and I were colleagues at the Air Force Institute of Technology in the late 1970s. We jointly developed the instrument reported on in this book and jointly conducted some of the early validation studies (Chapters 2 and 3 of this book). He deserves a great deal of credit for the intellectual bridge between decision modeling and the study of motivation.

Some of the chapters in this book were coauthored and could not have been written without the assistance of the coauthors. Adrian Harrell coauthored Chapters 2 and 3. David Grigsby (Clemson University) coauthored Chapter 7. Anil Gulati (Clemson University) coauthored Chapters 7 and 9. William Hendrix (Clemson University) coauthored Chapters 9 and 10. Jay Coleman (Clemson University) coauthored Chapters 9 and 10, and analyzed most of the samples in this book. George Dostal of the Atlanta Falcons and Chet Zalesky of the University of South Carolina deserve a note of thanks for their help in collecting the data on football players for Chapter 12. David Christiansen of Police Consultants in Westmont, Illinois, helped perform the study on policemen documented in Chapter 13. Maria Eugenia Fonseca Mora of the University of Panama and Mahmoud Yasin and Anil Gulati of Clemson helped with the international study reported in Chapter 14. Thanks are due to all of the above for their contributions.

Ryan Amacher, dean of the College of Commerce and Industry at Clemson University, deserves a note of thanks. By granting this department head release time from teaching in the spring and summer of 1985, he allowed me to focus writing this book.

The manuscript could not have been word-processed and re-word-processed without the help of several. Alfreda Bouyer, my secretary, deserves a special thanks. While performing all of her regular and demanding duties as administrative assistant and head secretary in one of the largest departments on campus, she typed the majority of this book. Robin Stengel typed several of the chapters and tolerated my multiple revisions. My three daughters, Lisa, Shelly, and Debbie, researched and word-processed the extensive bibliography in the summer of 1985. I deeply appreciate their help and commitment to the book when faced with the distractions of MTV, swimming, and waterskiing.

I owe a very special acknowledgment to my wife, Barbara. When I was faced with the decision of undertaking this project, she encouraged me to proceed. Even though the combination of her work schedule and mine often leaves us precious little time together, she understood my marriage to the book. I appreciate her encouragement, understanding, and willingness to share me.

Michael J. Stahl
Clemson University

Contents

Part II
Managerial and Technical Motivation

Part III
Other Occupations and International Aspects

Part I
Theory and Instrument Development

1 The Theory and Applications of Need for Achievement, Need for Affiliation, and Need for Power

INTRODUCTION

Popularity of Three Needs

One of the most widely accepted theories of motivation since about 1960 is a trichotomy of needs theory popularized by Professor David C. McClelland of Harvard University. Many organizational behavior textbooks today discuss McClelland's need for achievement (n Ach), need for affiliation (n Aff), and need for power (n Pow)—for instance, Hampton, Summer, and Webber (1982); Luthans (1985); Steers (1981); Szilagyi and Wallace (1983). The three needs have been found to possess predictive power in a wide variety of settings, especially organizational ones.

McClelland's theorizing became popular in the early 1960s because of his pioneering work correlating n Ach with levels of economic/business progress in several cultures (McClelland 1961, 1962a). He found that n Ach behavior could be learned, and reported that an increase in the entrepreneurial behavior of small businessmen in India occurred after they received n Ach training (McClelland and Winter 1969). A considerable body of literature has developed relating n Ach to many behaviors/outcomes in which the individual works toward accomplishing moderately difficult goals through his/her individual effort. Managerial effort, sales performance, engineering design activities, academic success, and entrepreneurial activities are a few of the examples that come to mind (McClelland 1965a, 1979b; McClelland, Atkinson, Clark, and Lowell 1976; Singh 1978).

More recently McClelland has focused research on n Pow and its associated behaviors (McClelland 1975b). Part of that research has dichotomized n Pow into two dimensions or "faces of power" (McClelland 1970). Social or positive power, that is, influencing others for the sake of social, group, or organizational goal accomplishment, has been found to be a characteristic of effective managers and leaders (McClelland 1970). Personal or negative power, that is, controlling/directing others for the sake of demonstrating personal dominance or superiority, has been associated with fighting, sexual conquest, and excessive drinking (McClelland 1975b; McClelland, Davis, Kalin, and Wonne 1972). Recent empirical work has associated n Pow (especially the positive face of power) with executive behavior and effectiveness (McClelland and Burnham 1976; McClelland and Boyatzis 1982) as well as with stress (McClelland 1979a).

Of the three motives, n Aff has received the least attention. Notable exceptions are the works of Schachter (1959), McClelland and Burnham (1976), and McClelland and Boyatzis (1982). Schachter (1959) noted the importance of n Aff in development and maturation processes. McClelland and Burnham (1976) noted that excessive n Aff prevents managers from dealing with subordinates objectively.

Spectrum of Motivational Theories

Several content theories of motivation have been popular. Herzberg's two-factor theory (Herzberg, Mausner, and Synderman 1959) and Maslow's need hierarchy theory (Maslow 1943) were prominent. A shortcoming of many content theories is their neglect of a basic concept of psychology: individual differences. Many content theories specified that *all* people possess the same motives; they are motivated in the same way; or they follow the same developmental hierarchy.

The process theories of motivation, which recognize individual differences, are at the other end of a motivational theories spectrum. Prominent among the process theories is expectancy theory (Vroom 1964). Process theories argue that no two individuals are motivated by the same needs or the same perceptions of organizational rewards. Therefore, the researcher must examine the individual's perceptions and needs in order to offer a prediction of behavior. Because they are *so* flexible and *so* mathematically complex (Stahl and Harrell 1981, 1983), process theories are very difficult to operationalize. Therefore, they offer little power to predict behavior.

McClelland's theory lies between the content theories and the process theories. He recognizes the effect of learning and reinforcement history on motive acquisition and strength. Indeed, he refers to the three needs as socially acquired needs (McClelland 1975b). Because his theories recognize individual differences and have specified content—that is, three needs—the theory offers considerable promise of explanatory power.

DEFINITIONS AND MANIFESTATIONS

Need for Achievement

The term "high achiever" has widespread usage in the vernacular. However, the theory of n Ach offers a specific definition and associated set of behaviors. N Ach has been defined as goal directed behavior where the goal is moderately difficult—that is, there is a reasonable chance of success—and the individual is provided with specific feedback about personal performance (McClelland 1961, 1962b, 1966; McClelland, Atkinson, Clark, and Lowell 1976). Because of the absolute dedication to goal accomplishment of the high need achiever, he/she will put forth almost whatever effort is required to meet the objective if detailed feedback is provided on progress toward its accomplishment. Since the goal must be one in which the person's own effort is related to goal accomplishment, extremely high levels of n Ach are associated with individual activities. Common examples are sales, engineering research, academics, individual sports, and entrepreneurial activities. Moderately high levels of n Ach may be found where the link between individual effort and goal accomplishment is not quite so strong, such as team activities, team sports, and managerial activities.

N Ach has two separate bases or may be manifested in two separate ways. Both a hope of success and a fear of failure result in achieving behaviors (McClelland, Atkinson, Clark, and Lowell, 1976; Yamauch and Doi 1977). Although one dimension may be thought of as a positive orientation and the other as a negative orientation, both result in achieving behaviors. One can surmise the early childhood experiences and parental reinforcement practices that yield the two separate manifestations. Positive reinforcement is associated with hope of success. Punishment or negative reinforcement may be associated with fear of failure. Because of this link, fear of failure may not yield the extremely high levels of n Ach associated with hope of success.

Need for Power

Similarly, n Pow may be manifested in two separate ways. Both hope of influence and fear of powerlessness are tied to n Pow (McClelland 1975b). Fear of powerlessness may cause one to assume a leadership position because he/she does not want someone else to be in control.

In the culture of this country, it is unfortunate that the term "need for power," or "power motivation," has a distasteful or pejorative connotation (McClelland 1970). The rugged individualism inherent in our society, our distaste for monarchs dating back to the American Revolution (as manifested in the Declaration of Independence), the checks and balances on power in the Constitution, and bad experiences with such powerful others as Adolf Hitler and Joseph Stalin may all be associated with the pejorative connotation. McClelland (1975b) related this negative connotation to one of the two faces of power, the negative or personal face of power. However, the reader should not forget that there is also a positive or social face of power associated with group or organizational influence/leadership and goal accomplishment. Indeed, this dimension of n Pow is the essence of organizational leadership (McClelland 1975b).

N Pow may be defined as influencing the activities or thoughts of a number of individuals (McClelland 1970, 1975b; McClelland and Burnham 1976). Examples may be found among politicians, military officers, clergy, managers, and executives. Indeed, some researchers report that n Pow is the single most potent characteristic discriminating between successful and nonsuccessful managers (Steger, Manners, Bernstein, and May 1975).

Need for Affiliation

The third of McClelland's trichotomy of needs is n Aff. It is defined as establishing and maintaining friendly relationships with others (Schachter 1959; McClelland and Burnham 1976). It is observed in group activities and interpersonal relationships. Indeed, a person high in n Aff can be very frustrated if placed in a job that requires isolation from others—whether the isolation is geographical or psychological. For this reason, McClelland and Burnham (1976) and McClelland and Boyatzis (1982) argued that high n Aff is not associated with effective managerial leadership. Friendships with some subordinates prevent the manager from dealing with all subordinates objectively. Indeed, McClelland and Burnham (1976) argued that "good guys make bum bosses."

N Aff has two separate dimensions or manifestations. It may arise from either a hope of inclusion or a fear of rejection (Decharms 1957; Schachter 1959). Either dimension causes the individual to behave so as to please others or to not offend others. Since managers must sometimes be very directive in their work, even to the point of taking disciplinary action, a person who is overly concerned with pleasing or not offending others will experience role conflict as a manager. Examples of high n Aff may be found in the helping professions, such as nursing and the clergy. The only example found where n Aff had a positive organizational outcome was a study by Dalton and Todor (1979), in which n Aff was positively associated with effectiveness for union stewards.

APPLICATIONS

Career Counseling

Given the above descriptions and findings in various jobs, it is apparent that one application of the trichotomy of needs is in career and vocational counseling. Since various jobs require different levels of n Ach, n Aff, and n Pow, and since McClelland (1981) argues that the needs are formed in childhood and subsequently change slowly, young people could be advised in high school or college on appropriate jobs to match their motivational profiles. It makes no sense to advise a person low in n Ach to be a salesperson or an engineer.

Selection

From an organizational perspective, an application is in the selection of employees. The selection of managerial talent and of technical talent are two specific examples. Those examples are mentioned for two reasons. First, studies have been performed demonstrating the importance of these needs for these two occupations (Stahl 1983, 1986). Second, managers and technical employees are frequently difficult and expensive to recruit. They can be very costly to the organization if their performance is low or if their tenure is short-lived.

Training and Job Assignment

Another organizational application is in training and job assignment. McClelland and Winter (1969) found that n Ach could be reinforced and strengthened through intensive training. Indeed, Szilagyi and Wallace (1983) noted that n Ach is the easiest of the three motives to train. They also noted, as did Steger (1978), that n Pow is almost impossible to train. Therefore, a person who is considering a change to a job requiring frequent n Pow behaviors but scores low in n Pow—for instance, a high-achieving engineer considering a change to a managerial position—could be counseled against the job move.

MEASUREMENT

If the theory is so powerful, why should this book be written? If the uses are as potent as suggested above, why don't more organizations select, train, and assign on the basis of n Ach, n Aff, and n Pow?

Thematic Apperception Test

To be sure, McClelland is a superb theoretician and conceptualizer. However, most of the empirical work associated with the three needs has thus far been performed with the Thematic Apperception Test (TAT), a projective test in which the person is asked to write stories about pictures that are provided. The stories are subsequently content-analyzed by a scorer for n Ach, n Aff, and n Pow themes. Comprehensive literature reviews by Clarke (1972), Entwisle (1972), and Fineman (1977) demonstrate that such a measurement approach contains much measurement error, and is unrealiable and invalid. The literature reviews argue against further use of the TAT. Indeed, most organizations will not use an assessment device in personnel decisions that is not reliable and valid. Fineman (1977) also noted measurement problems with many questionnaire approaches to measuring the needs.

An Alternative Measurement Approach

Impressed by the ability of the three needs to explain behavior, especially in organizational contexts, and aware of the measurement problems associated with the TAT and several other questionnaire approaches, a search was started for an alternative measurement approach. Given the particular interest of organizational use, the search and design efforts focused on a measurement approach for adults. This book reports on those design efforts, validation of the instrument, and use of the instrument in organizational settings.

A huge intellectual debt to McClelland is acknowledged. The purpose of this research is not to change or challenge his theory. Rather, it is to apply his theory with much greater measurement reliability and validity. In such a fashion, it is hoped that organizations and researchers can more fully use n Ach, n Aff, and n Pow to model and predict behavior.

2 A Preliminary Decision Modeling Approach for Measuring Achievement, Affiliation, and Power

DECISION MODELING

In 1960 P. J. Hoffman (p. 130) suggested that "hypotheses concerning personality correlates" could be tested by examining mathematical models of the behavior exhibited by decision makers. More recently Zedeck (1977) and Mitchell and Beach (1977) suggested that the behavioral decision theory modeling approach should be used to investigate human motivation. The last two articles were very influential in guiding this research.

This research approach is based conceptually on the Brunswik lens model (Brunswik 1952), which has been widely used to study human decision-making behavior. Comprehensive reviews of the literature have been published by Einhorn and Hogarth (1981); Hammond, Rohrbaugh, Mumpower, and Adelman (1977); Kaplan and Schwartz (1975); Libby (1981); Slovic and Lichtenstein (1971); and Slovic, Fischhoff, and Lichtenstein (1977).

This chapter is coauthored by Adrian M. Harrell of the University of South Carolina and Michael J. Stahl. It is adapted from A. M. Harrell and M. J. Stahl, "A Behavioral Decision Theory Approach for Measuring McClelland's Trichotomy of Needs," *Journal of Applied Psychology*, 1981, Vol. 66, pp. 242–247. Copyright (1981) by the American Psychological Association. Adapted by permission of the publisher and the authors.

A principal advantage of this approach for the investigation of human motivation is that it allows hypotheses to be examined on the basis of the actual decision-making behavior exhibited by subjects, rather than on subjects' self-reports of their motivation. Indeed, Arnold and Feldman (1981) showed that decision modeling measures of motivation are not subject to social desirability response biases frequently found in self-report measures.

METHOD

The Instrument

McClelland (1961, 1975b) described some of the characteristics of n Aff, n Pow, and n Ach in the context of the kind of job a person would be expected to seek. With this in mind, a decision-making exercise was constructed that asked each subject to indicate the likelihood that he or she would seek each of a number of hypothetical jobs. An example of one such job from the exercise is contained in Table 2.1.

TABLE 2.1. An Example Decision

This job involves . . . .

    Establishing and maintaining friendly relationships with other persons . . . . Fairly Often

    Influencing the activities or thoughts of a number of individuals . . . . Rarely

    Accomplishing difficult (but feasible) goals and later receiving detailed information about your personal performance . . . . Very Often

    If all other factors (pay, location, etc.) were the same, about what chance is there you would seek this job?

0%   10%   20%   30%   40%   50%   60%   70%   80%   90%   100%

Definitely no   Definitely yes

The exercise instructions directed each subject to assume that he or she was seeking a new position and that a number of jobs were available. All of these jobs were essentially alike in pay, benefits, location, and so on, differing only in the degree to which the three key activities were involved. These activities were establishing and maintaining friendly relationships with other persons (n Aff); influencing the activities or thoughts of a number of individuals (n Pow); and accomplishing difficult (but feasible) goals and later receiving detailed information about one's personal performance (n Ach). The activities occurred either rarely, fairly often, or very often in each of the various jobs. These three factors served as the information cues that were provided to each subject on which to base his or her job choice decisions. The wording of the three cues was derived from a review of McClelland's (1961, 1962a, 1975b, 1979b) descriptions of the three motives. Since three possible frequencies of occurrence and three different information cues were involved, each subject was required to reach 27 job choice decisions (3^3 = 27, a full factorial design).

The Samples

Three population groups were sampled in the course of the study. All but a few of the subjects in each group were males.

The decision-making exercise was distributed to 347 relatively junior Air Force officers who were full-time graduate students majoring in either management or engineering at the Air Force Institute of Technology, the resident graduate school of the Air Force. There were 156 completed and usable instruments returned. Some demographic data, along with each individual's graduate grade point average (GGPA) and recent officer performance appraisal scores, were also collected. The average respondent's GGPA was 3.56 with a standard deviation of .32. Performance evaluation scores averaged 1.80, with a standard deviation of .82; these values ranged from 1.0 (outstanding) to 3.0 (average). In general, the respondents were in their middle to late 20s, were lieutenants or captains, and had been in the Air Force about 5–7 years.

The exercise was also distributed to 475 scientists and engineers at a large Air Force research and development laboratory. From these, 173 usable instruments were completed and returned. The average respondent was 35 to 39 years old and was a federal civil servant in grade level GS–13. These subjects also indicated how many papers they had published in professional/technical journals during the preceding year. Goodman, Rose, and Furcon (1970) established the validity of self-reported publication counts. The distribution of the reported publications was nearly exponential, with about three-fourths of the respondents indicating no publications during the preceding year. The mean was .24, with a standard deviation of .62. This distribution corresponds to that reported by Stahl and Koser (1978) for another Air Force research and development laboratory, so no reporting bias seems evident.

The exercise was also distributed to an entire class (174 members) of executive grade Air Force officers attending the Air War College at Montgomery, Alabama. Officers who attend the Air War College have been formally identified by the Air Force as individuals who possess the potential for promotion to very senior military rank. The Air War College executives completed and returned 95 usable instruments. The average respondent was about 40 years old, had served in the Air Force for 20 years, and either had been promoted recently to colonel or was a senior lieutenant colonel. Virtually all of these officers reported outstanding performance appraisal scores, as would be expected from such a carefully identified group.

Hypotheses

Eight directional hypotheses were derived from statements in the previously cited writings of McClelland to guide the initial validation effort:

1. N Ach is the dominant motive for the graduate students.

2. N Ach is the dominant motive for the scientists and engineers.

3. N Pow is the dominant motive for the military executives.

4. The military executives are lower in n Ach than the other two groups of subjects.

5. The military executives are higher in n Pow than the other two groups of subjects.

6. There is a positive association between student GGPA and n Ach.

7. There is a positive association between officer performance appraisal scores and n Pow.

8. Scientists and engineers who have published during the preceding year are higher in n Ach than those who have not.

RESULTS

Initial Analysis

A multiple regression model was derived for each subject based on the 27 decisions the individual reached. Interaction terms did not account for a substantial portion of the variance, and consequently were discarded. The model used was

$$\text{Job Choice} = B_1 \, (\text{Aff}) + B_2 \, (\text{Pow}) + B_3 \, (\text{Ach}).$$

The factorial design used in the exercise resulted in three independent variables in the above model being uncorrelated with each other. As a result, the numerical size of the standardized regression coefficient (beta weight) associated with each independent variable indicates the weight each subject placed on each of the decision cues in arriving at his or her job choice decisions (Darlington 1968; Ward 1962). With this in mind, each of these beta weight values was treated as a numerical score whose size was indicative of the strength of an individual's n Aff, n Pow, and n Ach in examining the hypotheses presented earlier.

The average individual squared multiple correlation coefficient (R^2) obtained from the regression analysis was .69, which suggests that the subjects were reasonably consistent decision makers. Those subjects whose individual R^2 values did not indicate a statistically significant overall regression model ($p < .05$), or who did not place a significant weight on a cue ($p < .05$), were not used in the subsequent analysis. This procedure resulted in only about 5 percent of the total sample being discarded, which suggests that most subjects completed the self-administered exercise with little difficulty. One hundred forty-nine graduate students, 161 scientists and engineers, and 94 military executives were therefore included in the final analysis results presented below.

Validity

The summarized data for hypotheses 1–5 are contained in Table 2.2. Hypotheses 1, 2, and 3 were all supported by the data. N Ach was higher than both n Pow and n Aff for both the student and the scientist and engineer groups ($p < .01$). N Pow was higher than both n Ach and n Aff for the military executive group ($p < .01$). Hypotheses 4 and 5 were also supported by the data. The military executives had lower n Ach scores than did the students or the scientists and engineers ($p < .01$). They also had higher n Pow scores than the individuals in either of the other groups ($p < .01$).

TABLE 2.2. Three Need Scores by Subject Group, Hypotheses 1–5

Need	Scientists & Engineers (n = 161)		Graduate Students (n = 149)		Military Executives (n = 94)	
	M	SD	M	SD	M	SD
n Ach	.46	.32	.48	.31	.33	.38
n Pow	.29	.33	.31	.29	.45	.22
n Aff	.30	.31	.36	.30	.36	.26

M = mean; SD = standard deviation.

Hypotheses 6, 7, and 8, which involve concurrent validity issues, were also supported by the data. There was a significant, positive correlation between student GGPA and n Ach ($r = .20$, $p < .05$). In addition, students whose grades qualified them to be considered as distinguished graduates (GGPA of at least 3.75) had higher n Ach scores than did their classmates (two sample t test, $p < .05$). Graduate students' n Pow scores exhibited a significant, positive correlation of .38 ($p < .01$) with their officer performance appraisal scores. Those scientists and engineers who reported that they had published during the preceding year scored higher in n Ach than those who did not publish during that period (two sample t test, $p < .05$).

DISCUSSION

This chapter proposes a new approach for measuring McClelland's trichotomy of needs. The new approach is derived from behavioral decision theory. It involves modeling individuals' decision-making behavior to determine how persons weight their n Aff, n Pow, and n Ach in arriving at job choice decisions. A decision-making exercise was employed to gather the empirical data, which were collected from graduate students, scientists and engineers, and military executives. Multiple regression analysis was used to determine how each subject weighted the three needs in arriving at his or her job choice decisions.

The results of the initial research are encouraging, as all eight hypotheses used to guide the research effort were supported by the empirical data. However, the research effort described here is only one step in the overall process required to demonstrate a measurement instrument's validity. The reliability of the decision-making instrument must be established, and convergent/discriminant validity studies must be performed.

With these cautioning remarks in mind, it is believed that the new approach does possess a number of positive characteristics. The decision-making exercise is easy to understand and can be completed quickly. The subjects in the study described here received only the written instructions provided with the exercise, which was self-administered. About 15–20 minutes were required for completion, including the questions used to gather the information used in the initial validation effort. In addition, the job choice scenario used in the decision-making task is a realistic situation with which most persons must sometime contend.

A multiple cue decision-making task was used. This means that the subjects were required to arrive at some implicit weighting of the three cues (needs) to achieve the level of decision-making consistency required for a statistically significant multiple regression model to result. An individual was not, however, required to provide an explicit self-report of the importance of the needs. Consequently, the issue of whether the needs are "conscious" or "unconscious" (Fineman 1977; McClelland 1975b, p. 6) was avoided. Furthermore, the new approach allows the measurement of all three needs simultaneously, using multiple regression analysis.

Although the research effort described here was exploratory in nature, the results do provide positive support for the belief expressed by Mitchell and Beach (1977) and by Zedeck (1977) that the behavioral decision theory modeling approach can be effectively used to study human motivation.

3 Validation of a Refined Decision Modeling Approach to Achievement, Power, and Affiliation

The average individual squared multiple correlation coefficient (R^2) for the initial decision modeling approach reported in Chapter 2 was .69 across all subjects. Conversely, there was 31 percent unexplained or error variation that limited the reliability or consistency of the instrument. The authors hoped to decrease the unexplained variation through modifications to the original approach. This chapter extends the original research by reporting on evolutions of the original behavioral decision theory measurement approach, reliability data, convergent-discriminant validity results, a social desirability test, further criterion related validity tests, and further group difference construct validity tests across seven samples.

HYPOTHESES

Prior study and research (Arnold and Feldman 1981; Bedeian and Hyder 1977; Clarke 1972; Entwisle 1972; Fineman 1977; Harrell and Stahl 1981; McClelland 1961, 1970, 1975b, 1979b; McClelland

This chapter is coauthored by Michael J. Stahl and Adrian M. Harrell. It is adapted from M. J. Stahl and A. M. Harrell, "Evolution and Validation of a Behavioral Decision Theory Measurement Approach to Achievement, Power, and Affiliation," *Journal of Applied Psychology*, 1982, Vol. 67, pp. 744–751. Copyright (1982) by the American Psychological Association. Adapted by permission of the publisher and the authors.

and Burnham 1976; McClelland, Atkinson, Clark, and Lowell 1976; McClelland and Winter 1969; Schachter 1959; Schnieder and Green 1977; Winter 1973) led the authors to test 15 specific hypotheses:

1. Test-retest reliabilities are statistically significant.

2. There are no significant associations among social desirability and the three needs.

3. In a convergent-discriminant validity study, there are positive associations between each of the three respective motives and nonsignificant correlations among unlike motives as measured by this approach and another approach to the three needs.

4. N Ach is the dominant motive for graduate students.

5. N Pow is the dominant motive for management executives.

6. Management executives are higher in n Pow than the other groups in this study.

7. Graduate students are higher in n Ach than the other groups in this study.

8. A positive association exists between high school academic record and n Ach.

9. A positive association exists between high school leadership activity and n Pow.

10. A positive association exists between the number of hours spent studying and n Ach.

11. A positive association exists between the number of hours spent with friends and n Aff.

12. College students who held a campus student office score higher in n Pow than those who did not.

13. A positive association exists between grade point average (GPA) and n Ach.

14. A positive association exists between the number of people supervised and n Pow.

15. There are no differences in n Ach, n Pow, and n Aff between the sexes.

This chapter tests these hypotheses with a refined decision modeling measure called the Job Choice Exercise (JCE).

METHOD

Samples

Seven different samples from a variety of organizations were used in this research.

Sample 1: High school seniors. Thirty college-bound high school seniors in a Midwestern suburban high school completed the JCE. Approximately half were females.

Sample 2: Academy cadets. The JCE was given to the entire freshman class at the United States Air Force Academy in June 1980. Within a week of their arrival, 1,564 cadets completed the exercise as part of a longitudinal turnover study. Ninety of the instruments had data missing and were not usable. In addition to the JCE scores, the Academy registrar's office provided some demographic data. Each cadet's high school academic record, which is his or her high school class rank expressed as a percentage and adjusted for class size, and the cadet's high school activity index, which measures his or her position of responsibility and leadership in high school adjusted for class size, were provided. The prior academic record had a mean of 1,078.4 and a standard deviation of 133.7. Each cadet's overall academic GPA, as recorded by the Academy after the first year's study, was also provided (M = 2.99, SD = .70).

Sample 3: Management undergraduates. The third sample consisted of 75 junior and senior administrative management students at Clemson University. In addition to the JCE, several demographic questions were asked and the Crowne-Marlowe (1960) Social Desirability Index (M = 14.35, SD = 4.41) was administered. Self-report measures were gathered of the average number of hours per day the subject spent studying outside of class (M = 3.23, SD = 2.53), the average number of hours per day the subject spent with friends outside of class (M = 4.93, SD = 2.53), and whether the student held at that time, or had ever held, a campus student office (such as fraternity/sorority president, class officer, campus club officer). Twenty-three responded "yes," and 52 said "no." Forty-six males and 29 females were in the sample. The JCE was given a second time to 45 in this group three weeks after the first administration, to examine test-retest reliability.

Sample 4: Accounting undergraduates. The fourth sample consisted of 46 senior undergraduate accounting students at the University of South Carolina. Fifteen female and 31 male subjects were in the sample. The cumulative GPA was also gathered for these students (M = 3.18, SD = .50).

Sample 5: MBA students. The fifth sample consisted of 103 graduate students in business (MBA) at the University of South Carolina. Thirty worked part-time, 39 worked full-time, and 28 of the 39 held supervisory positions. The supervisors were asked how many people they supervised (M = 15.3, SD = 29.3). All 69 who worked completed the Steers and Braunstein (1976) Manifest Needs Questionnaire, which measures n Ach, n Aff, n Autonomy, and n Dominance for subjects who hold a job. The means and standard deviations were as follows: n Ach, 26.64 and 2.80; n Aff, 20.01 and 2.61; n Aut, 19.71 and 3.51; and n Dom, 23.46 and 3.16. There were 75 males and 28 females. Eighty-five of the 103 completed the JCE four weeks after the first administration.

Sample 6: Officer graduate students. The sixth sample consisted of 31 Air Force officers who were graduate students in management at the Air Force Institute of Technology. The officers were captains with 4–11 years' service.

Sample 7: Accounting partners. The seventh sample consisted of 11 partners in one of the "Big Eight" accounting firms that has an office in the Southeast. The partners were the senior higher ranking people in the firm, as there were several hierarchical levels below them. Their income and their rank in the organization marked them as successful executives.

Measure

The wording of each of the cues for n Aff, n Pow, and n Ach was the same as in the original version reported in Chapter 2. However, the cue levels were changed from three (very often, fairly often, and rarely) to two (very high [95 percent] and very low [5 percent]). The wording of the decision (Decision A) was revised to conform more closely to the idea of valence (Stahl and Harrell 1981; Vroom 1964). The measurement methodology was the same: Regression of the Decision A values on the three cues yields three standardized regression coefficients (beta weights) that represent n Aff, n Pow, and n Ach. Table 3.1 contains one of the jobs from the revised measure. (A copy of the complete instrument is in the Appendix.)

TABLE 3.1. Job Choice Exercise (JCE) Example: Job #1

In this job, the likelihood that a major portion of your duties will involve
—establishing and maintaining friendly VERY
 relationships with others is . . . . HIGH (95%)
—influencing the activities or thoughts VERY
 of a number of individuals is . . . . LOW (5%)
—accomplishing difficult (but feasible) goals
 and later receiving detailed information about VERY
 your personal performance is . . . . HIGH (95%)

DECISION A. With the factors and associated likelihood levels shown above in mind, indicate the attractiveness of this job to you.

-5	-4	-3	-2	-1	0	+1	+2	+3	+4	+5

Very   Very
Unattractive   Attractive

FURTHER INFORMATION ABOUT JOB #1: If you exert a great deal of effort to get this job, the likelihood that you will be successful is **MEDIUM (50%)**.

DECISION B. With both the attractiveness and the likelihood information presented above in mind, indicate the level of effort you would exert to get this job.

0	1	2	3	4	5	6	7	8	9	10

Zero effort   Great effort
to get it   to get it

©M. J. Stahl and A. M. Harrell, 1981.

The Further Information and Decision B were added to the original instrument to test separate propositions about Vroom's (1964) motivation model (Stahl and Harrell 1981). However, in their research the authors found, from the comments of many subjects, that these two additions made the n Aff, n Pow, and n Ach purpose of the instrument less transparent to them. Many said that they thought the purpose of the instrument was to study how they incorporated probabilistic information into their second decision (Decision B). Therefore, the authors have left Further Information and Decision B in the instrument as distractors. These two items are in no way used to compute the n Aff, n Pow, and n Ach scores from regressions of the Decision A values on the three cues.

The basic design is a full factorial with each of the three cues at two levels, for a total of eight basic jobs (2 x 2 x 2). Since the Further Information is presented at three levels (5 percent, 50 percent, 95 percent), a triple replicate of a 2^3 yielded a total of 24 values of decision A (3 x 2 x 2 x 2). In addition to the 24 jobs associated with the triple replicate of the three cues at two levels, six additional jobs were added at the front of the decision-making exercise as warm-up decisions. These additional six jobs are not used in the computation of the three need scores. Their only purpose is to allow the subject to become familiar with this innovative methodology before the 24 scored values of Decision A. Thus, the complete JCE has 30 jobs, 24 of which are scored.

Procedure

The method of administration differed across the seven samples. Samples 1, 3, 4, 5, and 6 completed the JCE during regular class hours. The cadets in sample 2 were assembled for a special testing session. The accounting partners in sample 7 completed the JCE at their leisure, as part of a job performance study, and mailed the instrument to one of the authors. Eleven of the 14 partners in the firm participated.

Since the method of administration differed, the same written instructions were included with each copy of the JCE. The instructions asked the subject to assume that he or she was seeking a job and that all other job outcomes—for example, pay and hours worked—were the same across all 30 jobs. The only way in which the hypothetical jobs differed was in accord with the information provided. These detailed written instructions were meant to put the subjects in the same frame of reference. Therefore, there was no need in any of the seven samples for the person administering the JCE to explain the exercise itself other than to comment that it was part of a turnover study or part of the authors' research.

Analysis

A multiple regression model was computed for each subject based upon his or her 24 decision A's and the three additive cues. The values of Decision A as provided by the subject, which ranged from −5 to +5, were used. For the regressions, the cue values of very high (95 percent) and very low (5 percent) were recoded to +1 and −1, respectively, to preserve orthogonality. Since interaction terms among the cues accounted for only a small percent of the explainable variance and were statistically significant for only some of the subjects, and since many other decision researchers have found simple additive models to account for most of the explainable variance (Slovic and Lichtenstein 1971; Slovic, Fischhoff, and Lichtenstein 1977), interaction terms were not included in the analysis. Again, the standardized regression coefficient (beta weight) is the motive score. As the authors came to realize that a low motive may have as much meaning as a high motive, they henceforth retained all beta weights from significant regression equations. This contrasts with Chapter 2, where nonsignificant beta weights were discarded.

The average individual R^2 resulting from the regression analyses is a measure of internal consistency reliability for such a decision modeling measure (Stahl and Harrell 1981). The average individual R^2 is a measure of how consistently the subjects implemented their decision-making policies in completing the instrument. In some samples there were a few decision makers who provided random data. Their R^2s did not even reach statistical significance at the .05 level, that is, an R^2 of .315. Those random decision makers were deleted from further analysis. This ability to operationalize individual consistency and to identify the subjects with the random data must be regarded as a strength of this approach to measurement.

Since some of the authors' hypotheses were tested in multiple samples, some of the findings were subjected to a meta-analysis (Glass 1976; Glass, McGaw, and Smith 1981). A meta-analysis, which refers to the statistical analysis of analyses, is particularly appropriate if a large collection of findings is mixed, or if a distribution of results has been achieved (Glass 1976; Glass, McGaw, and Smith, 1981). In the "Results" section below, a meta-analysis is performed if mixed findings are noted across many analyses.

RESULTS

Reliability

Two concepts of reliability were used to examine the reliability of the instrument. The first is consistency across time and the second is internal consistency.

The first concept of reliability was operationalized as test-retest reliabilities for samples 3 and 5. The scores at time 1 were correlated with the scores at time 2. Table 3.2 contains the results. These reliabilities, which are all significant ($p < .001$) and average .82, indicate a high degree of reliability over time.

TABLE 3.2. Test-Retest Reliabilities

Need	Management Undergraduates (n = 45)	MBA Students (n = 85)
n Aff	0.76	0.89
n Pow	0.76	0.85
n Ach	0.89	0.79

TABLE 3.3. Average R^2 by Sample

Sample	No. of Random Regressions	No. of Significant Regressions	Average R^2
High school seniors	0	30	.80
Academy cadets	24	1,450	.77
Management undergraduates	1	74	.78
Accounting undergraduates	1	45	.75
MBA students	3	100	.81
Officer graduate students	0	31	.82
Accounting partners	0	11	.81

The second concept of reliability is internal consistency, as measured by the average individual R^2. The average R^2s reported in Table 3.3, ranging from .75 to .82 and averaging .77, speak well of the internal consistency of the decision makers and of the refined instrument.

Validity

The second research issue concerned the social desirability content or bias of n Ach, n Pow, and n Aff. The correlations between the Crowne-Marlowe Social Desirability Index and n Aff, n Pow, and n Ach were .11, .10, and .09, respectively. For the 74 subjects, all three correlations were not significantly different from zero. This indicates that the JCE is not subject to a social desirability bias.

The convergent-discriminant validity study was performed with 69 subjects from sample 5 who held a job, as the Steers and Braunstein Manifest Needs Questionnaire requires subjects who are currently working. The correlations are in Table 3.4. As is apparent, the like needs are significantly associated with each other on both instruments. However, the correlations are not strong. Conversely, the unlike needs are not significantly correlated among themselves.

TABLE 3.4. Convergent-Discriminant Validities
(n = 69)

Manifest Needs Questionnaire	Job Choice Exercise		
	n Aff	n Pow	n Ach
n Aff	0.24*	0.11	-0.15
n Dominance	-0.06	0.34*	-0.02
n Ach	-0.15	-0.05	0.33*

*$p < .01$.

Hypotheses 4, 5, 6, and 7 were examined via the sample profiles on the motives. Table 3.5 contains the means and standard deviations of the samples for n Aff, n Pow, and n Ach.

**TABLE 3.5. Distributions of n Aff, n Pow, and n Ach
for the Seven Samples**

Sample	n	n Aff	n Pow	n Ach
High school seniors	30			
M		.56	.18	.47
SD		.23	.34	.26
Academy cadets	1,450			
M		.49	.31	.46
SD		.27	.29	.26
Management undergraduates	74			
M		.52	.32	.44
SD		.21	.26	.32
Accounting undergraduates	45			
M		.50	.27	.44
SD		.23	.33	.28
MBA students	100			
M		.33	.35	.57
SD		.35	.28	.24
Officer graduate students	31			
M		.28	.49	.62
SD		.26	.16	.21
Accounting partners	11			
M		.34	.57	.48
SD		.28	.18	.19

M = Mean; SD = standard deviation.

Paired sample t tests were used to examine hypotheses 4 and 5, whereas two sample t tests were used for hypotheses 6 and 7. The n Ach was the dominant need for both samples 5 and 6. The n Ach was higher than n Aff and n Pow for the 100 MBA students and for the 31 Air Force officer graduate management students ($p < .01$). N Pow was the dominant need for sample 7. The accounting partners' n Pow scores were higher than their n Aff ($p = .05$) and their n Ach scores ($p < .05$). Their n Pow scores relative to those of the other samples supported hypothesis 6. N Pow for the accounting partners was substantially higher than the first five samples' n Pow scores ($p < .01$), and marginally higher than the Air Force officers' ($p < .1$). N Ach was higher for the graduate students' samples than the executives ($p < .01$) and the other samples ($p < .05$).

The eighth and ninth issues, which involved the cadets' high school behavior, were both supported. There was a significant correlation between high school academic record and n Ach (r = .06, p < .001). N Pow displayed a significant correlation with high school leadership index (r = .05, p < .001). Neither correlation is high in an absolute sense. However, recognition of the sample size behind the correlations, the diverse nature of the nationwide sample, and the diversity of the activities that are normalized by one standard index at the Academy places the correlations in perspective.

Hypotheses 10, 11, and 12, which concerned the behavior of undergraduate students, were all supported. There was a positive correlation between n Ach and the number of hours spent studying (r = .23, p < .05). A significant correlation was found between the number of hours spent with friends and n Aff (r = .22, p < .05). Those students who held a campus student office scored significantly higher in n Pow (M = .41) than those who did not hold an office (M = .28, p < .05).

The relationship between GPA and n Ach was supported in both tested samples. There was a significant correlation between n Ach and first year GPA for the cadets (r = .12, p < .01), and a significant correlation between n Ach and cumulative GPA for senior undergraduates in sample 4 (r = .26, p < .05).

A positive association between the number of people supervised and n Pow (r = .28, p < .05) was observed in sample 5. This finding supported hypothesis 14.

The last issue, concerning sex differences, was tested across samples 2–5. No differences between the sexes were found on n Aff, n Pow, or n Ach for samples 3, 4, and 5. No difference between the sexes was found on n Aff and n Pow for the cadets. However, the female cadets scored significantly higher than the males on n Ach (M = .51 vs. .44, p < .01). A meta-analysis (Glass 1976; Glass, McGaw, and Smith 1981) of these 12 sex-difference analyses was performed to determine if 1 apparently significant finding out of 12 could have occurred by chance. Under the assumptions of a binomial distribution and a p = .01 for each test, the probability of 1 out of 12 tests indicating significance by chance is .11. In other words, the single "significant" finding out of 12 could have occurred by chance. Therefore, one concludes no apparent differences in n Aff, n Pow, and n Ach between the sexes.

DISCUSSION

The purposes of this chapter are to report on evolutions of the original behavioral decision theory measurement approach to n Aff, n Pow, and n Ach described in Chapter 2, and to further test the psychometric properties of the new approach. Modification of the original design, which contained three levels for each of McClelland's motives in a full factorial design with 27 decisions, to a new design, which contains two levels each for n Aff, n Pow, and n Ach in a triple replicate of a full factorial with 24 scored decisions, 24 filler decisions, and 6 warmups seems to have paid off. The reliability and validity data reported herein are supportive of the new design.

The calculated reliabilities, both in terms of internal consistency (R^2s around .8) and test-retest reliabilities (r's around .8) are better than the low reliabilities (r's around .3) Entwisle (1972) reported for a frequently used measure of these motives, the TAT. The JCE was also found to be free of a social desirability bias. Comparison with the Steers and Braunstein (1976) measure indicated the preferred pattern of convergent and discriminant validities, although the convergent validities were not strong. Criterion related validities and group difference construct validity tests also supported the beta weight measures of n Aff, n Pow, and n Ach.

From a methodological viewpoint, one must note the increase in the average individual R^2 from .69 in the first version of the JCE (Chapter 2) to .77 for this version (p < .001). Although there are only 24 scored decisions in this version of the JCE, in contrast with 27 scored decisions in the first version, the cue levels are more precisely described, that is, very high (95 percent) or very low (5 percent). This lends credence to Libby's (1981) comment that dichotomizing cue levels and precisely describing their levels can decrease noise. The use of six warm-up decisions in this version of the JCE may also have helped.

Our research was stimulated in part by Clarke's (1972) and Entwisle's (1972) criticisms of the low reliability associated with the TAT. Subsequently, Fineman (1977) comprehensively reviewed the psychometric properties of the TAT and several other measures of n Ach. He concluded that other projective measures of n Ach suffered from low reliabilities, just as Clarke (1972) and Entwisle (1972) had noted for the TAT. Fineman's (1977) literature review also indicated that some of the questionnaire based instruments contained items that are unrealistic for working managers. Therefore, our research was meant to follow the suggestions of Clarke (1972), Entwisle (1972), and Fineman (1977) to design a reliable measure of n Aff, n Pow, and n Ach for working personnel. The design reported herein is also appropriate for people who might soon be seeking a job (such as students).

Part II
Managerial and Technical Motivation

4 Identifying Managerial Motivation on the Basis of Achievement and Power Motivation

MANAGERIAL MOTIVATION

Much of McClelland's earlier emphasis was on n Ach as it relates to managerial/entrepreneurial behavior and economic achievement (McClelland 1961, 1979b; McClelland, Atkinson, Clark, and Lowell 1976; McClelland and Winter 1969). Characteristic of the earlier work on managerial behavior, McClelland commented: "At least at the lower levels, n Achievement seems to contribute to managerial success in large U.S. companies" (1961, p. 269). More recently the work of McClelland has focused on n Pow as it relates to managerial/ executive behavior and effectiveness (McClelland 1970, 1975b; Mc-Clelland and Burnham 1976). "This finding confirms the fact that power motivation is important for management" (McClelland and Burnham 1976, p. 103). The combination of these two needs as a measure of managerial motivation is the subject of this chapter.

In a widely cited and well researched book on managerial behavior and performance, Campbell et al. (1970) devoted an entire chapter to the subject of managerial motivation. In a job/task analysis of what effective managers actually do, the authors noted the frequency of behavior aimed at influencing others (n Pow) and the frequency of

This chapter is adapted from M. J. Stahl, "Achievement, Power and Managerial Motivation: Selecting Managerial Talent with the Job Choice Exercise," *Personnel Psychology*, 1983, Vol. 36, pp. 775–789. Adapted with permission.

behavior concerned with setting and accomplishing goals (n Ach). To characterize effective (as distinguished from noneffective) managers, they remarked: "Better managers tend to show a lifetime pattern of high achievement, power and economic motivation" (Campbell et al. 1970, p. 361). This view seems to be gaining acceptance, as evidenced by Steers's comment in an organizational behavior textbook: "Hence, based on these findings, it would appear that the most successful managers may be those who combine a power-orientation *with* an achievement-orientation" (Steers 1981, p. 76).

One of the most extensive treatments of the relationship of n Ach to n Pow is a chapter in a book of readings in honor of McClelland (Veroff 1982). "Achievement motivation directs people to meeting socialized standards of excellent performance and thus to highly efficient task-centered strivings, whereas power motivation directs people to doing whatever draws most attention to their own effect on the world. The two motives seem to be fused in instances where the standard of excellence is to win in a social competitive activity or to solve a problem that will be given a great deal of recognition" (Veroff 1982, p. 100). Since problem solving by managers frequently is recognized by superiors, subordinates, and peers, and since managers frequently compete with other organizational units for resources or priorities, it appears that the managerial role provides multiple opportunities for the two motives to be fused.

Four empirical studies were found that specifically tested McClelland's motivation theories in managerial samples. Cummin (1967) tested a mixed sample of middle and top level managers and found that the more successful managers scored higher in n Ach and in n Pow than the less successful managers. N Aff did not discriminate between the successful and nonsuccessful in Cummin's (1967) study. Wainer and Rubin (1969) found that both n Ach and n Pow were significantly related to company performance for research and development entrepreneurs. However, n Aff was not significantly related to company performance. Varga (1975) reported that the simultaneous presence of both n Ach and n Pow was significantly correlated with research and development effectiveness for scientists, engineers, and executives. Varga did not investigate n Aff. McClelland and Boyatzis (1982) found that a combination of high n Pow and Low n Aff characterized long-term success for upper level managers, whereas a combination of high n Pow and high n Ach characterized effectiveness for lower level managers.

Based upon McClelland's theory, Campbell et al.'s (1970) analysis, Steers's (1981) proposition, Veroff's (1982) comments on the fusing of n Ach and n Pow, and the cited empirical research, this chapter hypothesizes that the presence of *both* high n Pow *and* high n Ach is indicative of high managerial motivation. Conversely, it is hypothesized that the lack of both motives is indicative of low managerial motivation.

METHOD

Analysis

Stahl and Harrell (1982) reported data for 1,741 respondents from nationwide samples who completed the JCE. For purposes of this chapter, high n Pow was regarded as a score greater than the overall mean, and high n Ach was greater than the overall mean reported by Stahl and Harrell (1982). Therefore, a subject who scored greater than 0.314 on n Pow *and* greater than 0.464 on n Ach was labeled high in managerial motivation. A subject who scored less than or equal to 0.314 on n Pow *and* less than or equal to 0.464 on n Ach was labeled low in managerial motivation. Others were labeled medium in managerial motivation.

Because of a desire to explicate the selection implications, especially for the high and low managerial motivation groups, and because of the categorical dichotomous nature of most of the dependent measures, tests of proportions were used. Means tests were used for the examination of the dependent measure that was nearly interval, that is, managerial performance. Indeed, McClelland and Boyatzis (1982) analyzed similar data for upper and lower level managers with similar categorical analyses. Correlations are also reported to indicate the strength of the relationships across all three levels of managerial motivation.

The Samples

The JCE was administered to five samples. The first sample was composed of three managerial subsamples from three different organizations, with no criterion data. The first subsample consisted of 18 managers in a large textile manufacturing firm in the Southeast. The respondents included the four lowest levels of management in the firm. One respondent was deleted because of a nonsignificant regression. Almost all of the respondents were male. The second managerial subsample consisted of 11 managers in a Northeastern surgical steel instrument manufacturing company. The managers spanned four managerial levels. The third managerial subsample consisted of 14 second level managers at a large, municipally managed airport in the West. These 42 managers constitute sample 1.

Sample 2 consisted of 25 blue collar employees of a vending machine company in the Southeast. One respondent was deleted due to a nonsignificant regression. The employees' job was to collect money, refill, and perform minor repairs on vending machines. The employees were strictly hourly and nonsupervisory. Most were male.

The third sample consisted of 10 supervisors and 24 nonsupervisors in a regional office of a large insurance company in the Southwest. Their jobs were clerical in nature, dealing with insurance claims. Nearly all of the respondents, both supervisory and nonsupervisory, were women. No random regressions were found.

The fourth sample was 26 line and staff managers from a divisional office of a large computer manufacturing and marketing firm in the Northeast. Their latest managerial performance appraisal scores from the firm's own numerical evaluation system were provided. The five point scale ranged from 1, which was anchored at Outstanding, to 5, which was anchored at Needs Improvement. Two random regressions reduced the sample size to 24.

The fifth sample consisted of 50 first, second, third, and fourth level managers from a Midwestern plant of a large chemical firm. Managerial promotion data were provided. Promotion to the third or fourth level of management in the firm was a measure of managerial success, because it marked one as a companywide resource. The first or second level promotion decision was made within the division (fourth level). However, the third and fourth level promotion decisions required judgments from the other divisions, the plant manager, and other plants. These decisions required much more intensive examination of the manager. Therefore, the criterion measure was being promoted to the third or fourth level of management or not being promoted to either of those levels. Promotion or managerial level is an often used measure of managerial success (Campbell et al. 1970; Cascio 1982).

RESULTS

As shown in Table 4.1, 26 of the 42 managers (62 percent) from the managerial sample exhibited high managerial motivation. Six of the 24 blue collar employees (25 percent) had high managerial motivation. A test of those two proportions supports the proposition that managers scored higher than nonmanagers in managerial motivation ($z = 2.89$, $p < .01$). None of the managers exhibited low managerial motivation, whereas 7 of the 24 blue collar employees scored low. A direct test of two proportions is not advisable because of a zero in the managerial proportion. However, one can conduct two separate binomial hypothesis tests of the null hypothesis that the proportion of subjects with low managerial motivation is zero in each sample. Obviously, with 0 of 42 managers in the low category, one cannot reject the null hypothesis of a 0 proportion of managers in the low category. However, with 7 of 24 nonmanagers in the low category, one can reject the null hypothesis of a 0 proportion among the nonmanagers ($p < .01$). Therefore, one concludes that the proportion of managers with low managerial motivation is less than the proportion of nonmanagers with low managerial motivation.

TABLE 4.1. Managerial Motivation, by Managerial Status

	Managerial Motivation			
Sample	Low	Medium	High	Total
Managers	0	16	26	42
Blue collar workers	7	11	6	24
Total	7	27	32	66

As an alternative way to test the data, the correlation between managerial motivation and the dependent variable was calculated. For this and subsequent correlations, low, medium, and high managerial motivation scores were coded as 1, 2, and 3, respectively. Nonmanagers were coded as 0 and the managers were coded as 1. The resulting correlation was 0.49 ($p < .01$). This supports the proportion tests by indicating that knowledge of managerial motivation yields knowledge of a person's status as a manager or a blue collar worker.

TABLE 4.2. Managerial Motivation, by Supervisory Status

Sample	Managerial Motivation			
	Low	Medium	High	Total
Supervisors	0	0	10	10
Nonsupervisors	11	13	0	24
Total	11	13	10	34

Table 4.2 contains the supervisory and nonsupervisory data that were gathered in one organization. With 10 of 10 supervisors scoring high in managerial motivation and 0 of 24 nonsupervisors scoring high in managerial motivation, support is found for the hypothesis that supervisors score higher in managerial motivation than nonsupervisors. The converse is true for low managerial motivation.

The correlation between managerial motivation and status as a supervisor or nonsupervisor was also calculated. Supervisors were coded as 1 and nonsupervisors were coded as 0. The calculated correlation of 0.85 ($p < .01$) indicates that the higher a subject scored in managerial motivation, the more likely the subject was to be a supervisor.

TABLE 4.3. Managerial Motivation, by Managerial Performance

Managerial Performance	Managerial Motivation			
	Low	Medium	High	Total
1	0	1	5	6
2	1	8	8	17
3	0	1	0	1
4 & 5	0	0	0	0
Total	1	10	13	24

Table 4.3 contains data on managerial performance. The average performance for those with high managerial motivation was compared with the average performance of the others. The average per-

formance of 1.62 for the 13 with high managerial motivation is significantly greater than the average performance of 2.00 for the 11 others (t = 1.95, p < .05); since 1 was the highest score. Since only one of these managers scored low in managerial motivation, there are insufficient data to test a hypothesis concerning low managerial motivation and performance.

The correlation between managerial motivation and performance was 0.36 (p < .05). The magnitude of the correlation is somewhat limited because of the restriction of range, with few subjects exhibiting low managerial motivation.

TABLE 4.4. Managerial Motivation, by Managerial Level

Managerial Level	Managerial Motivation			
	Low	Medium	High	Total
1 & 2	3	21	8	32
3 & 4	0	4	14	18
Total	3	25	22	50

Table 4.4 contains the data to test the hypothesis on managerial promotion. The proportion of managers with high managerial motivation who were promoted to level 3 or 4 (14 of 18, or 78 percent) is significantly greater than the proportion of managers with high managerial motivation who were at levels 1 and 2 (8 of 32, or 25 percent) (z = 3.61, p < .01). None of the level 3 or level 4 managers exhibited low managerial motivation, whereas three of the level 1 and level 2 managers scored low on managerial motivation. Therefore, two separate binomial tests were used. One cannot reject the null hypothesis of a zero proportion of level 3 and 4 managers with low managerial motivation. However, the null hypothesis of a zero proportion of level 1 and 2 managers with low managerial motivation can be rejected (p < .01). Therefore, the proportion of level 3 and 4 managers with low managerial motivation is less than the proportion of level 1 and 2 managers with low managerial motivation.

The correlation between managerial motivation and managerial level was calculated. For this correlation, levels 1 and 2 were recoded as 0, and levels 3 and 4 were recoded as 1. The resulting correlation was 0.50 (p < .01). Again, the magnitude of the correlation may be limited because of the few subjects with low managerial motivation.

From a methodological viewpoint, the reader may wonder about the procedure of requiring an n Pow score above the 50th percentile *and* an n Ach score above the 50th percentile to be classified as high in managerial motivation, and vice versa to be labeled as low in managerial motivation. Why not form variable linear combinations of the two separate needs as a function of the criterion? To address this question, several discriminant analyses were run to search for a linear combination of n Ach and n Pow to best differentiate among the groups. For managerial promotion, the composite high, medium, and low managerial motivation measure used in this chapter correctly classified promoted managers better than a linear combination of n Ach and n Pow. The opposite held for nonpromoted managers. For managerial performance, after separating the "1" performers from the others, the composite measure used in this chapter and a linear combination classified equally well. For the managers and blue collar workers, the managerial motivation measure correctly classified the managers about the same as the linear combination, but the nonmanagers worse than the opposite measure. For the supervisory and non-supervisory data, the composite measure used herein classified better than a linear combination. Because of the above empirical reasons, and because the selection implications of the high, medium, and low managerial motivation measure are so apparent, the composite measure used herein is preferable.

DISCUSSION AND CONCLUSIONS

Based upon these data gathered from five samples from several organizations in different parts of the country, support was found for the hypothesis that the presence of *both* high n Pow *and* high n Ach is indicative of high managerial motivation. Support was also found for the hypothesis that low scores in both needs is indicative of low managerial motivation.

Concerning high managerial motivation, there was a higher proportion of subjects with high managerial motivation among the managers than among the nonmanagers; there was a higher proportion of managers with high managerial motivation among the promoted managers than among the nonpromoted managers; there was a dramatically higher percentage of supervisors with high managerial motivation than nonsupervisors; and managers with high managerial motivation had higher managerial performance than others. The opposite held true for low managerial motivation, except for managerial performance, which was untestable due to insufficient data. Based upon the above results, a person who scores high on *both* n Pow *and* n Ach on the JCE can be categorized as high in managerial motivation. Similarly, a person who scores low on *both* n Ach *and* n Pow on the JCE can be categorized as low in managerial motivation.

The potential selection implications of these results are fascinating. Based upon the above managerial results, it appears that an organization should select its low and middle level managers from candidates who score high on *both* n Ach *and* n Pow. Conversely, it should *not* select managers from candidates who score low on both n Ach and n Pow. The correlations indicate that there is statistical power across the three levels in the managerial motivation measure. However, the concept of fusing the two motives, as discussed in Veroff (1982), and the proportion tests reported herein indicate that the high and low managerial motivation groups are most clear-cut.

The training/career counseling implications are also worth discussing. Candidates considering a managerial promotion could be scored in terms of n Ach and n Pow. If a candidate scores low in both, his or her managerial potential should be seriously questioned. The behaviors associated with high n Pow and high n Ach could be explained to the candidate in detail in management training sessions. McClelland (1981) notes that power motivation is very slow to change. Therefore, a candidate who is low in n Pow and n Ach should be dissuaded from pursuing a managerial career. The data and the theory indicate that organizations should select managers from candidates who score high in n Pow and n Ach.

A strength and a limitation must be mentioned. These findings arise from a variety of organizations in different parts of the country. However, all of the data are concurrent. Before an organization actually uses the JCE in personnel decisions, it would be prudent for it to conduct a longitudinal validation study with the JCE. Then the organization would be on firmer legal and personnel grounds in personnel decisions. Chapter 5 reports on such a longitudinal validation study.

It seems that Campbell et al. (1970) and Steers (1981) were correct when they remarked that better managers are high in achievement and power motivation. McClelland and Burnham (1976) asserted that "Power is the great motivator" for top level executives. However, it appears that high n Pow *and* high n Ach are motivators for low and middle level managers.

A cover story by *Business Week*, on January 21, 1985, was entitled "The New Corporate Elite: They're Changing the Face of U.S. Business." It names the "Business Week 50" as executives who are representative of the new elite. In describing their characteristics, the article stresses a combination of power/influence *and* entrepreneurial skills. If the article is correct, then the dual theme of both achievement *and* power should be reinforced for years to come.

5 Predicting Cadet Turnover and Performance at the Air Force Academy: A Longitudinal Application of Power and Achievement Motivation

Chapter 4 demonstrates with data from a number of samples that a combination of both n Pow *and* n Ach effectively serves as a measure of managerial motivation. However, there is a shortcoming to those data—all of them are concurrent. The data in this chapter are meant to overcome that shortcoming by presenting two year longitudinal turnover and performance data associated with the managerial motivation measure.

The subjects for this research were cadets at the United States Air Force Academy (USAFA). They were in training to become career Air Force officers. Indeed, the majority of military generals come from the ranks of the military academies. Because of their future roles as leaders, they provided an excellent pool for a study of longitudinal selection issues with the JCE. The USAFA setting afforded excellent experimental conditions in terms of a large, nationwide sample of cadets of the same age group, yet of both sexes and different minority backgrounds.

Several studies have been performed to analyze military turnover. Typically, the studies use attitude and opinion surveys, and a concurrent measure of career intention. Hom, Katerberg, and Hulin (1979)

_____

The views expressed in this chapter are those of the author and not necessarily those of the United States Air Force Academy.

provide a summary of many of those studies. Few studies use longitudinal turnover, or performance, or measures that can be used in a selection model. Butler, Lardent, and Miner (1983) are an exception. However, they used the Miner Sentence Completion Scale with all its psychometric problems (see Chapter 7). This chapter uses two year turnover data, two year performance data, and the JCE measures of n Ach and n Pow to determine if the JCE could be used as an instrument to select future military leaders from among 18 year olds.

METHODOLOGY

Measures

Managerial motivation scores were derived from the JCE, as described in Chapter 4. A subject who scored above the mean of 0.314 in n Pow *and* above the mean of 0.464 in n Ach was labeled high in managerial motivation. A subject who scored less than or equal to *both* means was labeled low. Other scoring subjects were labeled medium.

The USAFA provided data on minority status, sex, two year turnover, two year cumulative military performance average (MPA), and two year cumulative GPA. Nearly all of the turnover was voluntary. Based on prior results at the USAFA, 80–90 percent of the turnover in a four year program occurred by the end of the second year. The GPA was calculated, as at most universities, solely on the basis of academic grades: A = 4 points, B = 3 points, and so on. The MPA was the two year cumulative average of performance ratings assigned by active duty Air Force officers of the cadet's performance of military duties and potential as an Air Force officer. MPA was also on a 0–4 point scale.

In order to keep the multiple analyses consistent and interpretable for selection implications, all three criteria were analyzed as dichotomous variables. Turnover already was a dichotomous variable. MPA and GPA were each split at their respective means. A two year cumulative MPA greater than 2.856 was labeled high MPA, and a cumulative MPA less than or equal to 2.856 was labeled low MPA. Similarly, a GPA greater than 2.590 was a high GPA and a GPA less than or equal to 2.590 was a low GPA.

The Sample

The sample was the entire freshman class that entered the USAFA in June 1980. This group is referred to as the class of 1984. The JCE was administered a few weeks after their admission in a single administration. The cadets' JCE scores are described in Chapter 3.

RESULTS

Women and Minorities

One area of concern was whether the use of the JCE would impact upon the USAFA's admission of women and minorities. Therefore, tests were made to determine if women scored differently from men and if minorities scored differently from majorities for the class of 1984.

TABLE 5.1. Sex, by Managerial Motivation

Sex	Managerial Motivation			Total
	Low	Medium	High	
Women	24	94	67	185
	(13.0)	(50.8)	(36.2)	(13.0)
Men	202	618	412	1,232
	(16.4)	(50.2)	(33.4)	(87.0)
Total	226	712	479	1,417

Numbers in parentheses are row percents.
$X^2 = 1.56$.
Source: Data provided by author.

Of the 1,417 members of the class of 1984 with valid JCE records and complete demographic data, 185 were women. Table 5.1 indicates the distribution of men and women by their managerial motivation scores. An associated X^2 value of 1.56 with 2 degrees of freedom (df) indicates that there is no difference between men and women on their managerial motivation scores. Specifically, there is no evidence of a difference between the proportion of women with high managerial motivation (67 of 185, or 36.2 percent) and the proportion of men with high managerial motivation (412 of 1,232, or 33.4 percent) ($z = 0.76$).

TABLE 5.2. Minority Status, by Managerial Motivation

Minority Status	Managerial Motivation			Total
	Low	Medium	High	
Minority	38	110	61	209
	(18.2)	(52.6)	(29.2)	(14.7)
Majority	188	602	418	1,208
	(15.6)	(49.8)	(34.6)	(85.3)
Total	266	712	479	1,417

Numbers in parentheses are row percents.
$\chi^2 = 2.59$.
Source: Data provided by author.

Of these 1,417 respondents from the class of 1984, 209 were minority members: Blacks, Orientals, Hispanics, and Native Americans. Table 5.2 indicates the distributions of minorities and majorities by their managerial motivation scores. The associated χ^2 value of 2.59 with 2 df indicates that there is no difference between minorities and majorities on their managerial motivation scores. Concerning high managerial motivation, there is no evidence of a difference between the proportion of minority members with high managerial motivation (61 of 209, or 29.2 percent) and the proportion of majorities with high managerial motivation (418 of 1,208, or 34.6 percent) ($z = 1.52$).

Turnover

Table 5.3 contains the cumulative second year turnover results, by managerial motivation. As can be seen, there is a significant spread in the turnover rate as a function of managerial motivation. The 27

TABLE 5.3. Turnover, by Managerial Motivation

	Managerial Motivation			
Turnover	Low	Medium	High	Total
Stays	137	510	354	1,001
	(58.3)	(69.9)	(73.0)	(69.0)
Leaves	98	220	131	449
	(41.7)	(30.1)	(27.0)	(31.0)
Total	235	730	485	1,450

Numbers in parentheses are column percents.
$\chi^2 = 16.46$, p < .001.
Source: Data provided by author.

percent turnover rate of those scoring high in managerial motivation is significantly different from the 41.7 percent turnover rate of those scoring low in managerial motivation ($z = 4.08$, p < .001). The sample size is larger than in Tables 5.1 and 5.2 because the missing data on sex and minority status did not reduce the sample size on Table 5.3.

Military Performance

For the MPA and GPA analyses, the sample sizes are smaller than for the turnover analysis because a cadet who left during the first

TABLE 5.4. MPA, by Managerial Motivation

	Managerial Motivation			
MPA	Low	Medium	High	Total
Low	101	300	190	591
	(59.8)	(51.4)	(46.9)	(51.0)
High	68	284	215	567
	(40.2)	(48.6)	(53.1)	(49.0)
Total	169	584	405	1,158

Numbers in parentheses are column percents.
$\chi^2 = 7.93$, p < .02.
Source: Data provided by author.

year is not included in the second year cumulative MPA. Therefore, Tables 5.4 and 5.5 have slightly different sample sizes than Tables 5.1–5.3.

Table 5.4 contains the cumulative second year MPA data, by managerial motivation. The 53.1 percent of the high managerial motivation cadets who had high MPAs is a greater proportion than the 40.2 percent of the low managerial motivation cadets who had high MPAs ($z = 2.82$, $p < .01$).

Academic Performance

The same comments on sample size that were presented for the MPA analyses hold for the GPA analyses. Second year cumulative GPA was analyzed.

TABLE 5.5. GPA, by Managerial Motivation

	Managerial Motivation			
GPA	Low	Medium	High	Total
Low	90	263	172	525
	(53.3)	(45.0)	(42.5)	(45.3)
High	79	321	233	633
	(46.7)	(55.0)	(57.5)	(54.7)
Total	169	584	405	1,158

Numbers in parentheses are column percents.
$\chi^2 = 5.64$, $p < .06$.
Source: Data provided by author.

Table 5.5 presents the managerial motivation analysis for GPA. As in the prior analyses, a significant 2×3 table is noted. In addition, the percentage of cadets with high GPA and low managerial motivation profiles (46.7 percent) is less than the percentage of cadets with high GPA and high managerial motivation profiles (57.5 percent) ($z = 2.36$, $p < .01$).

CONCLUSION

After analyzing longitudinal data with second year turnover, MPA, GPA, and JCE scores for the entire class of 1984 at the USAFA, several conclusions are offered. Use of managerial motivation scores from the JCE to select cadets for admission to the Air Force Academy would produce the following results: Turnover would decline significantly; MPA scores would increase significantly; and GPA scores would increase significantly. Moreover, these results could be achieved without adversely impacting the selection of either women or minorities.

Analysis repeatedly showed that the most powerful differences in the JCE scores are between the high managerial motivation scores and the low managerial motivation scores. Those scoring high in managerial motivation consistently scored better than the low scorers on turnover, MPA, and GPA. Therefore, the selection implications are apparent. Select those who score high in managerial motivation and do not select those who score low in managerial motivation. Only if there are not enough high scorers in the cadet application pool should those scoring medium be selected.

The sex and minority difference tests indicate no bias in terms of sex or minority status if the JCE were used in a selection environment. The finding of no sex difference in JCE scores coincides with the findings in Chapter 3. The finding of no sex difference in managerial motivation scores also coincides with the findings of Ritchie and Moses (1983), who found no sex difference in managerial potential in a seven year longitudinal study.

The use of cadet turnover as a dependent variable in a study of managerial motivation is worth discussion. Those cadets who quit— and nearly all cadet turnover is voluntary—are choosing *not* to accept a leadership role. Those who stay are opting for a leadership role while at the USAFA and for career leadership and managerial roles in the Air Force as officers. These data demonstrate that JCE managerial motivation scores are associated with that choice.

6 The Early Identification of Managerial Motivation: Differences Between College Leaders and Nonleaders

EARLY IDENTIFICATION

Two separate themes have emerged in the motivational literature that make a separate treatment of this chapter's subject worthwhile.

First, there are some noteworthy studies that have argued conceptually, and have presented supporting empirical data, that it is possible to identify managerial talent prior to full time employment. These studies are typically conducted while the individual is in college. Miner (1977a) has pursued this theme with the Miner Sentence Completion Scale. However, serious psychometric issues haunt that instrument (see Chapter 7). Owens and his colleagues (Neiner and Owens 1985; Owens and Shoenfeldt 1979) have classified collegians by using biographical inventories. Their research focuses primarily upon creating typologies of people, and only partly touches upon the identification of managerial talent. Their biographical inventory is quite lengthy and time consuming, which would make its use in a selection mode somewhat cumbersome. Steger and his colleagues (1978) used a variety of instruments and appeared to show potential in their approach to the early identification of managerial talent. Unfortunately, their team disbanded and little continuing research on their results has been published. The preceding research programs indicate that the early identification of managerial talent is a fertile research area.

The second theme that makes this research topic of interest is Miner and Smith's (1982) assertion that managerial motivation has been declining among collegians. If it is declining, then measurement and identification of the smaller number of those collegians high in managerial motivation become even more important.

Because of the interest in this topic, this chapter pulls together several samples of collegians to investigate the issue. Specifically, the reliability of the JCE managerial motivation measure among collegians and differences among several student leader and nonleader groups are investigated.

THE SAMPLES

Some of the subsamples are individually discussed in other chapters for separate reasons. The subsamples are pulled together here to deal with the topic of this chapter in one place.

Senior Management Majors

The JCE was given to 20 seniors majoring in management who were taking a course in business strategy at Clemson University. Three weeks later they completed the JCE a second time. About half of the students were women.

Junior Management Majors

The JCE was given to 111 juniors majoring in management who were taking a course in principles of management at Clemson University. Three weeks later, 95 completed the JCE a second time. This sample is described in Chapter 7. These first two samples are used to test the test-retest reliability of the JCE among collegians.

Fraternity and Sorority Presidents

Two subsamples of Greek presidents were collected at two separate times for two separate studies, and are combined in this chapter. Thirteen fraternity presidents at Clemson University completed the JCE in 1981. They were in their junior or senior year. Chapter 7 describes 31 more fraterntiy and sorority presidents who completed the JCE in 1983. There were 16 males and 15 females among these juniors and seniors. These 44 presidents are combined for this sample.

Nonleaders

Two separate subsamples of engineering students, designated as nonleaders for this research, are combined for this sample. Twenty-four junior and senior engineering students completed the JCE in 1981. Most were males. Chapter 7 describes 26 junior and senior engineering students studied in 1983, 7 of whom were women. These 50 students comprise the nonleader sample. The methodology of using Greek presidents as leaders, and engineering students as non-leaders, was used by Steger, Kelly, Chouiniere, and Goldenbaum (1975) in one of their early identification studies.

Student Senators

Thirty-four student senators at Clemson University completed the JCE. This sample of 13 females and 21 males consisted of juniors and seniors.

RESULTS

In all the results, managerial motivation scores were derived as described in Chapter 4, that is, a combination of n Pow *and* n Ach. Specifically, if a person scored above the norm mean of 0.314 in n Pow, and above the norm mean of 0.464 in n Ach, then the person was scored high in managerial motivation. If the individual scored below both means, then he or she was scored low in managerial motivation. Others were scored medium in managerial motivation.

Table 6.1 contains the test-retest reliabilities for the first two samples. As can be seen from the correlations of the time 1 scores with the time 2 scores, the measures are quite stable, with an average reliability of 0.80. The seniors exhibited higher reliability than the juniors in n Pow, n Ach, and, consequently, managerial motivation. Because the seniors were in the process of interviewing for managerial

TABLE 6.1. Test-Retest Reliabilities

Motivation	Management Juriors (n = 95)	Management Seniors (n = 20)
n Aff	0.87	0.85
n Pow	0.75	0.93
n Ach	0.71	0.85
Managerial motivation	0.61	0.79

Source: Data provided by author.

jobs at the time these data were collected, their n Pow and n Ach scores may be more stable than those of juniors, who were still a year away from that career move.

The managerial motivation of the three groups is described in Table 6.2. The Greek presidents had the highest managerial motivation of the three groups. The percent of Greek presidents who scored high in managerial motivation (30 of 44, or 68 percent) is significantly greater than the percent of nonleaders who scored high in managerial motivation (8 of 50, or 16 percent) ($z = 5.20$, $p < .01$), and the percent of student senators who scored high (12 of 34, or 35 percent) ($z = 3.00$, $p < .01$). On the other end of the managerial motivation scale, the percent of Greek leaders who scored low (3 of 44, or 7 percent) is significantly less than the percent of nonleaders who scored low (10 of 50, or 20 percent) ($z = 1.89$, $p < .05$), and the percent of student senators who scored low (9 of 34, or 26 percent) ($z = 2.31$,

TABLE 6.2. Managerial Motivation, by Sample

Sample	Managerial Motivation			
	Low	Medium	High	Total
Greek presidents	3	11	30	44
Nonleaders	10	32	8	50
Student senators	9	13	12	34
Total	22	56	50	128

Source: Data provided by author.

p < .05). The typical Greek president's profile was high in managerial motivation.

TABLE 6.3. Average Needs, by Sample

Sample	Needs		
	n Aff	n Pow	n Ach
Greek presidents (n = 44)	0.45	0.48	0.51
Nonleaders (n = 50)	0.52	0.30	0.39
Student senators (n = 34)	0.31	0.46	0.25

Source: Data provided by author.

To determine the source of the differences, the n Aff, n Pow, and n Ach scores were calculated for the three groups, and are listed in Table 6.3. The Greeks were not significantly different from the non-leaders in n Aff, but were greater than the student senators (t = 2.33, p < .05). The Greeks were significantly higher than the nonleaders in n Pow (t = 3.00, p < .01), but not significantly different from the student senators. On n Ach, the Greeks scored significantly higher than both the nonleaders (t = 2.00, p < .05) and the student senators (t = 4.33, p < .01). The average profile of the Greek presidents was high in n Pow and in n Ach. The average nonleader was just average. The average student senator was high in n Pow and low in the other two motives. This last profile may be the politician's profile.

DISCUSSION AND CONCLUSION

The purpose of this chapter is to determine if managerial motivation can be identified at an early stage. The works of Miner (1977a), Neiner and Owens (1985), and Steger (1978) indicate that managerial motivation can be captured among collegians. However, there are measurement issues and other problems with those approaches that make their use in selection impractical. Consequently, this chapter used the JCE managerial motivation measure, developed and validated in Chapters 4 and 5, to test its psychometric properties and ability to identify managerial motivation among collegians.

The JCE scores were found to be quite reliable among collegians. Across two separate groups, the average test-retest reliability of the n Aff, n Pow, and n Ach scores was 0.83, and the average test-retest reliability of the composite managerial motivation measure was 0.70. Using three college samples (44 Greek presidents, 50 nonleaders, and 34 student senators), the JCE managerial motivation measure demonstrated that the fraternity and sorority presidents displayed significantly higher managerial motivation scores than the other two groups. Neither of the other two groups scored higher than the Greek presidents in either n Ach or n Pow.

Based upon the reliability and construct validity data, it appears that the JCE managerial motivation measure can be used to identify managerial motivation among collegians. Further research should include a longitudinal validation study in which collegians are measured on the JCE managerial motivation measure and followed for five or ten years. Such a study would determine the payoff of the early identification of managerial motivation.

7 Identifying Managerial Motivation with the Job Choice Exercise and the Miner Sentence Completion Scale

MINER AND McCLELLAND

Since 1960 Miner and his colleagues have explored managerial motivation from the vantage point of role motivation theory (Miner 1960, 1964, 1977a, 1978a, 1978b; Miner and Crane 1981; Miner and Smith 1982). Based upon an analysis of the roles that managers perform, Miner has specified seven dimensions or roles that he has used to discriminate between successful and nonsuccessful managers. The roles are Authority Figures, Competitive Games, Competitive Situations, Assertive Role, Willingness to Impose Wishes, Standing out from the Group, and Routine Administrative Functions.

It would appear that the McClelland and the Miner constructs are not independent. N Pow is conceptually similar to Willingness to Impose Wishes, and n Ach may be related to Competitive Games and Competitive Situations. Indeed, Miner remarked: "Of the motivational theories, McClelland's views on achievement and power motivation appear to be the most conceptually similar and thus the most

This chapter is coauthored by Michael J. Stahl, David W. Grigsby, and Anil Gulati, all of Clemson University. It is an expanded version of M. J. Stahl, D. W. Grigsby, and A. Gulati, "Comparing the Job Choice Exercise and the Multiple Choice Version of the Miner Sentence Completion Scale," *Journal of Applied Psychology*, 1985, Vol. 70, pp. 228–232. Copyright (1985) by the American Psychological Association. Adapted by permission of the publishers and the authors.

likely to yield overlapping results. It would seem that although the McClelland and role-motivation formulations may be partially over-lapping, they are not likely to account for identical variance" (1978b, p. 757).

This research has two purposes: first, to examine the reliability and other psychometric properties of the JCE and the Miner Sentence Completion Scale; second, to compare the two formulations as measures of managerial motivation.

METHOD

Measures

Managerial motivation scores from the JCE were derived as described in Chapter 4. Specifically, a subject who scored greater than 0.314 on n Pow *and* greater than 0.464 on n Ach was labeled high in managerial motivation. A subject who scored less than or equal to 0.314 on n Pow *and* less than or equal to 0.464 on n Ach was labeled low in managerial motivation. Others were labeled medium in managerial motivation.

Most of Miner's work has been with a projective instrument known as the Miner Sentence Completion Scale (MSCS) (Miner 1978b). The most commonly used MSCS form is a free response form containing sentence stems that prompt the subject to complete the sentence. A scorer then scores the complete sentences for themes in concert with the seven Miner roles. As a projective instrument, the MSCS has encountered some of the reliability problems that the projective TAT has encountered. Brief, Aldag, and Chacko (1977) performed an extensive psychometric investigation of the MSCS, reported low reliability coefficients for the instrument, and cautioned against further use of it. Subsequently, Miner (1978a) discussed a multiple choice version of the MSCS. The multiple choice version addresses the same seven scales as the projective MSCS, but can be rigorously scored by a computer without content analysis by a scorer. Therefore, the multiple choice form should be more reliable. It is a 40 item measure including five filler items. There are five scored questions for each of Miner's seven constructs. Each item has six possible answers. Miner's (1977b) scoring guide indicates whether the chosen answers should be scored +1, 0, or –1. The five items that constitute a given scale are subsequently summed to yield a scale score. Miner's scoring instructions were programmed on an IBM 3033 computer with Statistical Analysis System instructions to ensure consistent scoring of all subjects.

The Crowne-Marlowe (1960) Social Desirability Index was also administered. It is a scale consisting of 24 true-false items. The higher the score, the more a subject's answers are prone to a social desirability bias.

Subjects

Three samples were involved. The first was used to examine the psychometric issues. The second and third were used to test for differing managerial motivation.

All three instruments were administered to 113 juniors taking a principles of management course in the business school at Clemson University. Two subjects were deleted due to random data on the JCE, that is, R^2s less than 0.315 (see Chapter 3). There were 46 females and 65 males in the sample. Three weeks after the first administration, 95 of the same students completed both the JCE and the MSCS. Again, the MSCS was administered first.

The second sample consisted of 31 presidents of fraternities and sororities. There were 16 males and 15 females. These 31 campus leaders were juniors and seniors. Both the JCE and the MSCS were completed by this sample.

The third sample, designated as nonleaders for the present study, consisted of 28 junior and senior engineering students. Two subjects were deleted due to random data on the JCE. Seven women were in this group of 26 campus nonleaders. Both the JCE and the MSCS were completed. This methodology of using fraternity and sorority presidents as a leader group and a sample of engineering students as a nonleader group was employed by Steger, Kelly, Chouiniere, and Goldenbaum (1975) to test a forced choice version of the MSCS.

RESULTS

The results are presented in six subsections. Both internal consistency reliability and test-retest reliability are presented, followed by the social desirability test, sex difference tests, the correlations between the MSCS and JCE, and tests between the leaders and non-leaders.

Internal Consistency

Since the JCE scores are derived by regressing the subjects' 24 decisions on the three criteria of n Aff, n Pow, and n Ach, a measure of the subjects' consistency in completing the decisions is the average individual squared multiple correlation coefficient (R^2) resulting from the regressions (see Chapters 2 and 3). The average individual R^2 for the 111 subjects was 0.79. In other words, there was 21 percent unexplained or error variation. This compares favorably with the average R^2 of 0.77 reported in Chapter 3 for 1,741 subjects.

TABLE 7.1. Internal Consistencies for MSCS and JCE (n = 111)

Measure	Reliabilities
MSCS	
Authority Figures	0.24
Competitive Games	0.16
Competitive Situations	0.33
Assertive Role	0.00
Imposing Wishes	0.00
Standing out from Group	0.00
Routine Administrative Functions	0.41
Total score	0.57
Average	0.21
JCE	0.79

The reliabilities for the MSCS are the coefficient alphas. The reliability for the JCE is the average individual R^2.

A measure of internal consistency for the MSCS scales is coefficient alpha (Nunnally 1967). Table 7.1 contains the coefficients for the seven MSCS scales. The alpha coefficients indicate that the MSCS scales are far from being internally consistent. The overall average coefficient alpha of 0.21 is far less than the minimum reliability coefficients of about 0.6 recommended by Nunnally (1967).

TABLE 7.2. Principal Components Analysis of MSCS (n = 111)

Principal Component Number	Eigenvalue	Percent of Explained Variance
1	2.67	7.6
2	2.22	6.3
3	2.00	5.7
4	1.99	5.7
5	1.72	4.9
6	1.66	4.7
7	1.54	4.4
8	1.46	4.2
9	1.45	4.2
10	1.35	3.9
11	1.25	3.6
12	1.20	3.4
13	1.10	3.2
14	1.07	3.1

Given such low alphas, the factor structure of the 35 MSCS questions was explored. Table 7.2 contains the results of the orthogonally rotated principal components analysis. Retaining factors with eigenvalues greater than 1.00 indicates that there are 14 factors in the 35 questions rather than Miner's concept of 7 scales. The loadings of the 35 questions on the 14 factors were confusing enough to prohibit interpretation.

Test-Retest Reliability

Table 7.3 presents the correlations of the time 1 scores with the time 2 scores for both the JCE and the MSCS. The reliabilities for the JCE, five of the MSCS scales, and the MSCS total score are satisfactory. However, the MSCS Authority Figures and Standing out from Group scales exhibited unsatisfactory test-retest reliabilities.

TABLE 7.3. Test-Retest Reliabilities
(n = 95)

Measure	Correlations
JCE	
n Aff	0.87
n Pow	0.75
n Ach	0.71
Managerial motivation	0.61
Average	0.74
MSCS	
Authority Figures	0.45
Competitive Games	0.69
Competitive Situations	0.63
Assertive Role	0.67
Imposing Wishes	0.61
Standing out from Group	0.41
Routine Administrative Functions	0.63
Total score	0.78
Average	0.61

TABLE 7.4. Social Desirability Analysis
(n = 111)

Title	Correlation with Crowne-Marlowe
JCE	
n Aff	−.04
n Pow	.00
n Ach	.03
Managerial motivation	.00
MSCS	
Authority Figures	.08
Competitive Games	−.03
Competitive Situations	.15
Assertive Role	.13
Imposing Wishes	.00
Standing out from Group	.16*
Routine Administrative Functions	.14
Total score	.04

*p = .05, one tailed.

Social Desirability

Of the 12 correlations computed (4 JCE scores and 8 MSCS scores) with the Crowne-Marlowe Social Desirability Index, only a single correlation in Table 7.4 indicated a social desirability bias. Standing out from Group was significantly associated ($r = .16$) with the Social Desirability Index.

Sex Differences

Twelve t tests were conducted to determine if there were differences between men and women in the scores. Table 7.5 contains those results. The men scored higher than the women in Competitive Games and Assertive Role. Also, in the Assertive Role scale the men

TABLE 7.5. Sex Differences Means Tests

	Mean		
	Men	Women	
Title	(n = 65)	(n = 46)	t
JCE			
n Aff	0.55	0.53	−0.44
n Pow	0.29	0.32	0.42
n Ach	0.42	0.47	1.00
Managerial motivation	0.00	0.00	.00
MSCS			
Authority Figures	0.57	0.72	0.46
Competitive Games	2.01	1.15	−2.71**
Competitive Situations	0.65	0.17	−1.32
Assertive Role[a]	0.69	0.07	−2.09*
Imposing Wishes	0.06	0.35	1.14
Standing out from Group	1.15	0.78	−1.63
Routine Administrative Functions	0.97	1.26	0.93
Total score	6.10	4.50	−1.52

[a]Unequal variances modified t tests.
*$p < .05$, two tailed.
**$p < .01$, two tailed.

had greater variance than the women. The case of unequal variances and the two cases of different means are noteworthy, given Miner and Smith's (1982) assertion of declining sex differences in MSCS scores. The JCE finding of no sex bias corresponds to the results of no JCE sex differences in Chapters 3 and 5.

Intercorrelations

Table 7.6 contains the correlations between the JCE and MSCS. Only Authority Figures is related to the JCE.

TABLE 7.6. Correlations Between the JCE and the MSCS (n = 111)

MSCS	n Aff	n Pow	n Ach	Managerial Motivation
Authority Figures	.00	.03	.19*	.19*
Competitive Games	.09	-.02	.10	.04
Competitive Situations	-.02	.09	-.08	.04
Assertive Role	-.02	.07	-.16	-.08
Imposing Wishes	-.15	.18	-.03	.18
Standing out from Group	.11	.08	-.02	.00
Routine Administrative Functions	.12	.02	-.09	-.09

*p < .05, two tailed.

Leaders and Nonleaders

The data for samples 2 and 3 are contained in Table 7.7. The means tests show four differences out of four on the JCE. The leaders scored lower in n Aff than the nonleaders, and higher in n Pow, n Ach, and overall managerial motivation than the nonleaders. Indeed, an examination of those who scored high in managerial motivation (a combination of high n Pow and high n Ach), as was done in Chapter 4, showed that the proportion of the leaders scoring high in managerial motivation (20 of 31, or .645) was significantly greater than the proportion of nonleaders who scored high in managerial motivation

TABLE 7.7. Leaders and Nonleaders Differences Means Tests

| Measure | Mean | | t |
	Leaders (n = 31)	Nonleaders (n = 26)	
JCE			
n Aff	0.43	0.56	-2.32*
n Pow	0.48	0.34	2.43*
n Ach	0.49	0.33	1.99*
Managerial motivation	0.58	0.08	3.03**
MSCS			
Authority Figures	0.10	0.12	-0.06
Competitive Games	3.36	3.04	0.85
Competitive Situations	1.29	-0.58	4.59**
Assertive Role[a]	0.90	0.19	1.68
Imposing Wishes	0.71	-0.23	3.20**
Standing out from Group	1.84	1.38	1.51
Routine Administrative Functions[a]	2.45	0.92	4.46**
Total score	10.65	4.85	5.63**

[a] Unequal variances modified t tests.
*p < .05, two tailed.
**p < .01, two tailed.

(6 of 26, or .231) (z = 3.14, p < .01). Four of the eight MSCS scales contained differences between the leaders and nonleaders. The leaders scored higher in Competitive Situations, Imposing Wishes, Routine Administrative Functions, and total score than the nonleaders.

DISCUSSION AND CONCLUSIONS

This research was prompted in part by Miner's (1978b) comment that n Ach and n Pow as theorized by McClelland ought to overlap conceptually with role motivation theory as formulated by Miner. These data indicate some overlap between n Ach and some of the MSCS scales. But little can be concluded from those correlations because they are based on MSCS scales too unreliable to support any conjecture about validity. Since reliability places an upper bound on validity (Nunnally 1967), the low test-retest reliabilities (an average of 0.61) and very low internal consistency reliabilities (an average of

0.21) indicate that the MSCS multiple choice scale measures much randomness. The reader may recall that Brief, Aldag, and Chacko (1977) reported troublesome reliabilities for the sentence completion version of the MSCS. The only MSCS score with reasonable test-retest consistency and internal consistency was the total score (0.78 and 0.57, respectively).

Steger, Kelly, Chouiniere, and Goldenbaum (1975) reported on a forced choice version of the MSCS using campus leaders and non-leaders, as in this research. Maybe that version is more reliable than either the multiple choice or the sentence completion version. However, the principal components analysis reported herein casts doubt upon the internal consistency of the seven constructs in the MSCS. Indeed, if one follows the suggestion of Cronbach and Meehl (1955), and views factor analysis as a test of construct valdity, then the seven MSCS constructs are in doubt. These factor analytic results seriously question the MSCS role motivation theory. Alternatively, if the theory is correct and if managers are motivated by the seven MSCS constructs, then one concludes that the seven scales simply do not measure the seven constructs. No other factor analytic studies of the MSCS were found. Therefore, future research should be devoted to further factor analytic studies of both the multiple choice and the free response versions of the MSCS.

The seven MSCS constructs are also questionable if one views the tests between the leaders and nonleaders as tests of construct validity (Cronbach and Meehl 1955). Four of the seven MSCS scales showed no difference between the leader and nonleader groups.

The JCE measure of n Ach, n Aff, and n Pow was shown to be quite reliable. Both the internal consistency estimate of 0.79 and the average test-retest reliability estimate of 0.74 speak well of its reliability. No social desirability biases or sex biases were apparent in the JCE. As a test of construct validity, four of the four JCE scores showed differences between the leaders and nonleaders. Most important, the overall managerial motivation score yielded differences (see Chapter 4). It is also interesting that the leaders scored higher in n Pow and lower in n Aff than the nonleaders. This is the pattern that McClelland and Boyatzis (1982) identified as a 16 year longitudinal predictor of success for upper levels of management (see Chapter 9).

8 Identifying Managerial and Technical Motivation Among Scientists and Engineers: An Assessment of Achievement and Power Motivation

MANAGERIAL VERSUS TECHNICAL MOTIVATION

What are the costs to an organization and to the individual if the organization promotes a productive scientist or engineer to a managerial job and the individual turns out to be an ineffective manager? The organizational costs include the lost professional productivity of the promoted individual as well as the diminished productivity and lessened morale of the group subordinate to the ineffective manager. The individual's costs include frustration and stress while he/she is in transition from a productive professional to an ineffective manager. What are the costs to a technically educated student if, after being counseled by an educational institution to seek a managerial job, the individual finds out on the job that he/she has little managerial talent? This chapter addresses the issue of identifying managerial talent among professionals by assessing managerial and technical motivation.

There are three separate n Ach and n Pow themes that need to be explored concerning managerial and technical motivation among scientists and engineers. First, a few studies have been performed that focused on n Ach and the performance of scientists (Helmreich, Beane, Lucker, and Spence 1978; McClelland 1954, 1956, 1962b).

This chapter is an expanded version of M. J. Stahl, "Selecting and Training Managerial Talent Among Scientists and Engineers: Power Motivates," *Research Management*, 1986. Adapted with permission.

These studies reported high levels of n Ach among scientists. Second, McClelland's work has focused on n Pow as it relates to managerial/ executive behavior and effectiveness (see Chapter 9). Characteristic of those studies, McClelland remarked: "Since managers are primarily concerned with influencing others, it seems obvious that they should be characterized by a high need for power, and that by studying the power motive we can learn something about the way effective managerial leaders work" (1975b, p. 254). Third, several studies have concentrated on *both* n Ach *and* n Pow as characteristics of managers (see Chapter 4).

The above three themes helped to form the primary research questions of this chapter. Does n Pow alone differentiate between managers and nonmanagers? Does n Ach alone differentiate between managers and nonmanagers? Are both motives higher in managers than in nonmanagers? The subjects for this research are managers high in n Ach because of their scientific and engineering backgrounds, and nonsupervisory scientists and engineers with high n Ach. Therefore, only n Pow is hypothesized to differentiate between the two groups.

THE SAMPLES

The JCE was administered to four samples of professional employees. The managers of the professional employees had scientific and engineering backgrounds.

The first sample was composed of 92 nonsupervisory engineers and scientists and 6 group leaders of those scientists and engineers. About half of the 98 had a master's degree in electronics, electrical engineering, mechanical engineering, or computer science. The other half had mostly a bachelor's degree, and a few had a doctorate. All were employed by a large electronic engineering design and development firm in the Southeast. This firm is referred to as organization 1 in this study.

The second sample consisted of 29 second, third, and fourth level managers and 22 nonsupervisory professionals from the nuclear division of a large chemical firm. The manager and nonmanager groups had been educated in chemical engineering, nuclear engineering, mechanical engineering, physics, or chemistry. Most had a bachelor's degree and a few had a master's degree. The firm is labeled organization 2. The 29 managers were the second, third, and fourth level managers from this organization reported in Chapter 4. The first line managers were not included in this chapter because many of them did not have scientific and engineering backgrounds.

The third sample was 26 line and staff managers from a divisional office of a large computer manufacturing and marketing firm in the Northeast. Two random regressions reduced the sample size to 24. These data are also discussed in Chapter 4. Their backgrounds were in computer science and electrical engineering. This firm is referred to as organization 3. Due to organizational constraints on data collection, it was not possible to gather nonsupervisory data.

The fourth sample consisted of 13 nonsupervisory professional employees in a large university computer center. Their educational background was in computer science. There were not enough managers with a scientific background at the site to compare with the 13 professionals. This organization is labeled organization 4.

RESULTS

In the ensuing tables, separate tests are made between the managers and nonmanagers within organization 1 and separate tests are made within organization 2. Organizations 3 and 4 are compared in Table 8.3. All the managers and nonmanagers across all four organizations are collapsed into two groups in Table 8.4.

As seen in Table 8.1, the managers exhibited higher power motivation than the nonsupervisory professionals in organization 1. No significant differences were observed between the two groups on the other two motives.

TABLE 8.1. Mean Motivations Between Managers and Nonmanagerial Professionals in Organization 1

Need	Managers (n = 6)	Nonmanagers (n = 92)	t
n Aff	0.44	0.30	1.01
n Pow	0.57	0.33	2.00*
n Ach	0.55	0.62	-0.57

*$p < .05$, two sample t test.

TABLE 8.2. Mean Motivations Between Managers and
Nonmanagerial Professionals in Organization 2

Need	Managers (n = 29)	Nonmanagers (n = 22)	t
n Aff	0.36	0.39	-0.46
n Pow	0.48	0.22	2.95**
n Ach	0.54	0.62	-1.02

**p < .01, two sample t test.

Table 8.2 shows a significant difference in n Pow between the managers and nonsupervisory professionals in organization 2. Again, no differences were observed in the other motives between the two groups.

Table 8.3 shows the same pattern as in Tables 8.1 and 8.2. However, it contains data across two organizations. The managers scored significantly higher than the nonsupervisory professionals in n Pow. No differences were observed on the other two motives.

As in Chapter 4, the managerial performance appraisal scores were correlated with the three need scores for the 24 managers in organization 3. A correlation of 0.36 (p < .05) between n Pow and managerial performance appraisal scores was observed. The other two correlations were not significant.

Table 8.4 contains the combined data for all four organizations. With the combined sample sizes, the differences are more apparent.

TABLE 8.3. Mean Motivations Between Managers and
Nonmanagerial Professionals in Organizations 3 and 4

Need	Managers (n = 24)	Nonmanagers (n = 13)	t
n Aff	0.21	0.40	-1.77
n Pow	0.53	0.21	3.02**
n Ach	0.55	0.54	0.16

**p < .01, two sample t test.

TABLE 8.4. Mean Motivations Between Managers and Nonmanagerial Professionals in Organizations 1, 2, 3, and 4

Need	Managers (n = 59)	Nonmanagers (n = 127)	t
n Aff	0.31	0.33	-0.38
n Pow	0.51	0.30	5.06**
n Ach	0.55	0.61	-1.49

**p < .01, two sample t test.

The managers scored substantially higher in n Pow than the others. No significant differences were observed for n Aff or n Ach.

One last test was performed on the data to determine if high scores in the composite managerial motivation measure (see Chapter 4) are found more frequently in managers of professionals than in nonsupervisory professionals. Using the JCE norms described in Chapter 4, a subject who scored greater than 0.314 on n Pow *and* greater than 0.464 on n Ach was labeled high in managerial motivation; one who scored less than or equal to 0.314 on n Pow *and* less than or equal to 0.464 on n Ach was low in managerial motivation; others were labeled medium in managerial motivation. Table 8.5 contains the data for the composite managerial motivation measure for all four organizations.

TABLE 8.5. Composite Managerial Motivation, by Organization

Organization	Group	Managerial Motivation			Total
		Low	Medium	High	
1	Managers	0	3	3	6
	Nonmanagers	6	51	35	92
2	Managers	0	11	18	29
	Nonmanagers	1	10	11	22
3	Managers	1	10	13	24
4	Nonmanagers	2	7	4	13
1-4	Managers	1	24	34	59
	Nonmanagers	9	68	50	127

Due to the low frequencies in the low managerial motivation category, it is not practical to perform difference tests in that category. Tests of proportions between managers and nonmanagers in the high managerial motivation category were performed. There was not a significant difference in organization 1 between the proportion of managers and nonmanagers exhibiting the high managerial motivation composite score. Neither was there a significant difference in organization 2. The same was true between the managers in organization 3 and the nonmanagers in organization 4. When the data were combined across the four organizations, the proportion of managers exhibiting the high composite managerial motivation score (34 of 59, or 0.58) was significantly higher than the proportion of nonmanagers exhibiting the high managerial motivation score (50 of 127, or 0.39) ($z = 2.41$, $p < .05$). However, the test was not very strong, considering that it was performed across all 186 subjects.

DISCUSSION AND CONCLUSIONS

This research was conducted partly because of three separate themes in the motivational literature. One theme referred to the notion that managers score higher than nonmanagers in n Pow. A second theme noted the high levels of n Ach in the scientific personnel. The third theme discussed high n Pow and high n Ach in managers. These data do indicate a high level of n Ach in both the managers with professional backgrounds and the nonsupervisory professionals. The high level of n Ach in the scientists and engineers does not differentiate them from the scientist or engineer promoted to a managerial job. That phenomenon could account for the lack of difference between the managers and nonmanagerial professionals in the n Ach and the weak difference in the composite managerial motivation score. Both groups were high, but not significantly different from each other, in n Ach. Technical motivation is dominated by n Ach. Tables 8.1 through 8.4 demonstrate that n Ach is dominant for the nonmanagers. Indeed, relative to the nationwide data collected by Stahl and Harrell (see Chapter 3) across 1,741 subjects and 7 samples, the managers' average n Ach was approximately in the 63rd percentile and the nonmanagers was in the 71st percentile. Both were high, but not different.

There were no differences in n Aff. Both were quite low. The average n Aff score for the managers was in the 27th percentile. The nonmanagers' average was in the 29th percentile.

The significant difference between the two groups was in n Pow. Strong support was found for the hypothesis that the managers of the professional employees scored higher in n Pow than the nonsupervisory professionals. This difference in n Pow was found from testing 59 managers of professional employees and 127 nonmanagerial professionals. The difference was found when tests were made within specific organizations and when the four organizations were collapsed in a single test. The average power motivation of the managers was in the 75th percentile, whereas that of the nonsupervisory professionals was in the 48th percentile. For managers with professional backgrounds, McClelland and Burnham (1976) are correct in their assertion that "Power is the great motivator." The managers with the professional backgrounds are already high in n Ach. This phenomenon reconciles these findings with those of Chapter 4, which discussed high n Pow and high n Ach among managers in different organizational settings.

Managerial performance appraisal scores were positively associated with n Pow for the managers in the one organization where those data were available. Such an association lends concurrent validity support to the n Pow measure.

The implications of these findings for identifying, selecting, counseling, and training managerial talent among scientists and engineers are worth discussion. The motivational profile for the non-managerial professional employee in research differs from that of the manager primarily in n Pow. This finding coincides with the finding of Steger, Manners, Bernstein, and May (1975), who described n Pow as a potent predictor of R & D managerial effectiveness. If a scientist or engineer is considering a promotion to a managerial position and he or she scores low in n Pow, the move should be questioned seriously. Since McClelland (1975b) defines n Pow as the essence of managerial leadership, and since McClelland (1981) also notes that n Pow is slow to change, a low n Pow scientist or engineer would be well advised not to make the move to the managerial ranks. If a personnel officer is attempting to identify candidates for managerial positions from among a number of professional employees, a test could be run for high n Pow. Since n Pow is slow to change and since many high technology organizations select managers of professional employees from within the ranks of currently employed professional employees, it seems that such organizations should choose managerial talent partly on the basis of existing n Pow. It is difficult to train n Pow because it is so slow to change.

There are skill bases for selection, such as technical skills and communication skills. However, these data indicate that the significant motivational basis for managerial selection among professional employees is n Pow. The costs mentioned in this chapter's first paragraph *can* be avoided.

9 Is Power the Great Motivator for Executives?: Testing Two Models of Power and Affiliation

EXECUTIVE MOTIVATION

The work of McClelland and colleagues has focused on n Pow and n Aff as they relate to executive behavior and effectiveness (Cornelius and Lane 1984; McClelland 1970, 1975a, 1975b, 1979a; McClelland and Boyatzis 1982; McClelland and Burnham 1976). An unresolved issue is that at least two alternative models of the relationship of n Pow to n Aff in executives may be found in the writings of McClelland.

The first model may be stated as "n Pow is greater than n Aff." References to this model are contained in McClelland and Burnham: "Moreover, the top manager's need for power ought to be greater than his need for being liked by people" (1976, p. 101). Two works by McClelland (1975a, p. 46, Table 1; 1975b) further reinforce this model.

The second model may be stated as "high n Pow and low n Aff." Interestingly, this second model is found in some of the same sources as the first. "The better managers we studied are high in power motivation, low in affiliation motivation, and high in inhibition" (McClelland and Burnham 1976, p. 103). McClelland (1975a, 1975b) reinforces this theme. Most recently, McClelland and Boyatzis (1982)

This chapter was coauthored by Michael J. Stahl, William H. Hendrix, Jay Coleman, and Anil Gulati, all of Clemson University.

slightly modify this model when they speak of moderate-to-high n Pow and low n Aff. Due to operationalization problems with the recent modification, the present research compares the two models "n Pow greater than n Aff" and "high n Pow and low n Aff" in several samples of executives and managers.

METHOD

Subjects

The JCE was administered to 47 senior Air Force officers who had recently been selected for promotion to the rank of colonel and were to attend the Air War College (AWC), the Air Force's senior service school. Promotion to colonel and selection to attend AWC is extremely selective. Less than 5 percent of Air Force personnel are chosen, and future general officers in the Air Force usually come from such a group. On the average, these executives grade officers were 41 years old and had 19 years of military service.

The JCE was also administered to 89 officers who had recently been promoted to major and selected to attend the Air Command and Staff College (ACSC), the Air Force's intermediate service school . Promotion to major is the first real competitive promotion for officers in the Air Force. Selection to attend ACSC identifies them as being at the top of the majors' promotion list. These individuals may be described as upwardly mobile. Their average age was 36 and they averaged 14 years in service. Two of the ACSC officers had nonsignificant JCE regressions and were deleted.

The JCE was also administered to 105 Air Force lieutenants and captains who were attending the Squadron Officer School (SOS), the Air Force's initial service school. Selection to attend SOS is noncompetitive. Their average age was 30 and they averaged 8 years in service. One of these SOS subjects was deleted due to a nonsignificant JCE regression equation.

The JCE was also administered to 311 first year cadets at the Air Force Academy, the Air Force's four year service academy. Future career oriented Air Force officers come from among these graduates. Their average age was 18. These data were gathered from the class of 1985.

The fifth sample consisted of 14 senior executives at the vice presidential, presidential, or chairman of the board level. Two chairmen of the board, three presidents, one executive vice president, one senior vice president, five division vice presidents, one vice president for manufacturing, and one vice president for personnel were included. They were in a variety of organizations, including manufacturing, financial, holding, and international firms located in the Southeast, Northeast, and Midwest. These executives' titles, positions in their organizational hierarchies, and numbers of subordinates identified them as successful senior executives.

The sixth sample, referred to as the managerial sample, was composed of three managerial subsamples with no criterion data. They are the managers described in Table 4.1. The first subsample consisted of 18 managers in a large textile manufacturing firm in the Southeast. The respondents included the lowest four levels of management in the firm. One respondent was deleted because of a nonsignificant regression. Almost all of the respondents were male. The second managerial subsample consisted of 11 managers in a Northeastern surgical steel instrument manufacturing company. They spanned four levels. The third managerial subsample consisted of 14 second level managers at a large, municipally managed airport in the West. These 42 managers constitute the managers' sample.

The last sample consisted of 25 blue collar employees of a vending machine company in the Southeast. One respondent was deleted due to a nonsignificant model. The employees' job was to collect money, refill, and perform minor repairs on vending machines. They were strictly hourly and nonsupervisory. Most were male. They are listed in Table 4.1.

Procedure

It is difficult to determine from reading the works by McClelland cited above exactly how to quantify the two models. Faced with the lack of specification and a desire to ensure that the results were not a function of model specification, the authors decided to operationalize the "high n Pow and low n Aff" model three different ways. The first two ways were arbitrary. One method was above and below the respective 50th percentiles. The second was above the 67th percentile and below the 33rd percentile. The third method was above the 73rd percentile and below the 27th percentile, as suggested by Guilford (1954, pp. 428–429), to increase personnel selection efficiency.

Using the overall means and standard deviations reported by Stahl and Harrell (1982) for 1,741 subjects from seven samples, the JCE scores were converted into percentiles. The model of "n Pow greater than n Aff" was operationalized as the n Pow percentile > n Aff percentile.

In coping with this specification issue, McClelland and Boyatzis used a decision rule based partly on ". . . his T score of n Power was greater than or equal to 45, and greater than or equal to his T score of n Affiliation. The T score for the n Power variable was set slightly below the mean of 50, to increase the number of cases in this category of special interest" (1982, p. 738). Their decision rule has elements of both models. Cornelius and Lane (1984) approached the issue by subtracting the z score for n Pow from the z score for n Aff. Their rule is similar to the second model in this chapter.

RESULTS

In order to describe the military samples, the distributions of their need scores are in Table 9.1. As expected, the more senior samples are associated with higher n Pow. Table 9.2 contains the results for the four military groups of the four models.

Tests of rank ordered correlations were used to examine a model across samples. After coding the Air War College as 1 because it was the highest ranking service school, ACSC as 2, SOS as 3, and the AFA as 4 to represent the lowest ranking military school, a perfect rank ordered correlation of 1.0 was observed with the proportion of the sample who fit the models. This correlation was observed for both the "n Pow > n Aff" model and the "high n Pow and low n Aff" model operationalized three different ways.

To examine how the "Pow > Aff" model compares with the managerial motivation model discussed in Chapter 4, the managerial motivation model scores are shown in Table 9.3. Relative to the percentages shown for the "Pow > Aff" model in Table 9.2, the managerial motivation model does not fare as well for the Air War College executives. The "n Pow > n Aff" model identifies 34 percent more of the Air War College executives. Also, the percentages across the samples who display high managerial motivation do not display the same transitivity as does the "n Pow > n Aff" model. Therefore, the "n Pow > n Aff" model is preferable as a way to describe a military executive profile.

TABLE 9.1. Distributions of Needs, by Military Sample

Needs	Air War College (n = 47)	Air Command & Staff College (n = 87)	Squadron Officer School (n = 104)	Air Force Academy (n = 311)
Aff				
M	.39	.38	.36	.49
SD	.21	.25	.29	.25
Aff percentile				
M	37	36	33	52
SD	25	25	27	27
Pow				
M	.58	.52	.43	.32
SD	.19	.21	.23	.27
Pow percentile				
M	82	76	66	51
SD	17	21	23	26
Ach				
M	.48	.49	.53	.49
SD	.23	.26	.29	.24
Ach percentile				
M	52	54	60	54
SD	28	27	28	27

Note: M = mean; SD = standard deviation
Source: Data provided by authors.

To describe the managerial samples, the distribution of their need scores are in Table 9.4. The 14 senior executives showed both the highest n Pow and the lowest n Aff of any sample in this book. Table 9.5 contains the managerial sample data for the model tests of n Aff and n Pow.

After recoding the senior executives to 1 as the highest ranking managerial sample, the managers to 2, and the blue collar workers to 3, a perfect rank ordered correlation of 1.0 was observed with the proportion who fit each model. This statement held true for both the "n Pow > n Aff" model and the "high n Pow and low n Aff" model operationalized three different ways.

The managerial motivation scores, which were computed as discussed in Chapter 4, are shown in Table 9.6. The high managerial motivation score for the senior executives does not identify them as

TABLE 9.2. Pow and Aff Models, by Military Sample

Sample	Pow > Aff	High Pow and Low Aff Using the 50th Percentile	High Pow and Low Aff Using the 33rd Percentile	High Pow and Low Aff Using the 27th Percentile
Air War College	41/47 (.87)	30/47 (.64)	17/47 (.36)	15/47 (.32)
Air Command & Staff College	69/87 (.79)	48/87 (.55)	29/87 (.33)	25/87 (.29)
Squadron Officer School	77/104(.74)	56/104(.54)	26/104(.25)	18/104(.17)
Air Force Academy	153/311(.49)	85/311(.27)	37/311(.12)	24/311(.08)

Note: The entries are the number in the sample who fit the model, divided by the sample size, followed by the ratio in parentheses.
Source: Data provided by authors.

TABLE 9.3. Managerial Motivation, by Military Sample

Sample	Managerial Motivation			Total
	Low	Medium	High	
Air War College	2(.04)	20(.43)	25(.53)	47
Air Command & Staff College	4(.05)	36(.41)	47(.54)	87
Squadron Officer School	9(.09)	44(.42)	51(.49)	104
Air Force Academy	45(.14)	158(.51)	108(.35)	311

Note: The entries are the number in the sample who fit the model, followed by the ratio in parentheses.
Source: Data provided by authors.

TABLE 9.4. Distributions of Needs, by Managerial Sample

Needs	Senior Executives (n = 14)	Managers (n = 42)	Blue Collar Workers (n = 24)
Aff			
M	.20	.33	.62
SD	.22	.18	.16
Aff percentile			
M	15	29	70
SD	19	18	19
Pow			
M	.61	.46	.18
SD	.21	.25	.26
Pow percentile			
M	85	69	32
SD	19	26	26
Ach			
M	.55	.61	.45
SD	.25	.17	.17
Ach percentile			
M	63	71	48
SD	27	21	21

Note: M = mean; SD = standard deviation.
Source: Data provided by authors.

TABLE 9.5. Pow and Aff Models, by Managerial Sample

Sample	Pow > Aff	High Pow and Low Aff Using the 50th Percentile	High Pow and Low Aff Using the 33rd Percentile	High Pow and Low Aff Using the 27th Percentile
Senior executives	14/14(1.00)	12/14(.86)	9/14(.64)	6/14(.43)
Managers	36/42(.86)	29/42(.69)	12/42(.29)	10/42(.24)
Blue collar workers	4/24(.17)	2/24(.08)	0/24(.00)	0/24(.00)

Note: The entries are the number in the sample who fit the model, divided by the sample size, followed by the ratio in parentheses.
Source: Data provided by authors.

TABLE 9.6. Managerial Motivation, by Managerial Sample

| Sample | Managerial Motivation | | | |
	Low	Medium	High	Total
Senior executives	0(.00)	5(.36)	9(.64)	14
Managers	0(.00)	16(.38)	26(.62)	42
Blue collar workers	7(.29)	11(.46)	6(.25)	24

Note: The entries are the number in the sample who fit the model, followed by the ratio in parentheses.
Source: Data provided by authors.

well as the "n Pow > n Aff" model does. The high managerial motivation score identifies only 9 of the senior executives, whereas the "n Pow > n Aff" model identifies all 14 of them. Nor does the managerial motivation measure discriminate among the three groups as well as the "n Pow > n Aff" model.

The last test was across all seven samples in Tables 9.2 and 9.5. Within each sample, a test of the "n Pow > n Aff" model vs. the "high n Pow and low n Aff" model showed a *higher* proportion supporting the first model in each sample. A sign test yielded a perfect statistic, as the "n Pow > n Aff" model had a higher proportion in each of the seven samples.

CONCLUSION

Both tests across samples for a given model and tests between models within samples indicated that "n Pow > n Aff" is the preferred model. All of the senior executives (14 of 14) and almost all of the AWC executive grade officers (41 of 47) showed the "n Pow > n Aff" pattern. The higher military rank and the higher executive rank were associated with higher proportions of subjects who possessed the "n Pow > n Aff" profile.

A limitation deserves mention. The method by which the two models were specified, using percentiles, guaranteed that whenever an individual satisfied the "high n Pow and low n Aff" model, he or she also satisfied the "n Pow > n Aff" model. A priori, the percent satisfying the "n Pow > n Aff" model must be greater than *or* equal to the percent satisfying the other models. Not only was this lower bound equality met, but for each of the seven groups, a *higher* proportion exhibited the "n Pow > n Aff" pattern than the "high n Pow and low n Aff" model. The fact that all seven exhibited a higher proportion mitigates the limitation. Therefore, this research supports McClelland and Burnham's comment that to be effective "the top manager's need for power ought to be greater than his need for being liked by people" (1976, p. 101). This research also generalizes the comment to include military executives as well as senior executives in industry.

This research was designed primarily to test a theory. However, there are certain applications apparent from the results. Managerial training, career counseling, and executive selection implications come to mind. Steger (1978) notes that need for influence is almost impossible to teach. Managers who view themselves as candidates for executive level positions could be exposed to these motivational profiles in managerial training sessions. If an individual's profile does not meet those found in this paper—specifically, if n Aff is greater than n Pow—the individual might consider a change in career plans, since these motives change very slowly (McClelland 1981). The selection implication is straightforward. These data demonstrate that an executive is almost never found with n Aff greater than n Pow. If a decision maker is considering several candidates for an executive level position, then a power > affiliation test could be used as a partial screen. Since power is the great motivator for executives, a candidate who is not motivated by power would be a rare success in the executive ranks.

The above comments are offered with a caution. The data on the managers and nonmanagers in Chapter 10 and on nurses in Chapter 11 indicate that age is not significantly associated with n Aff, n Pow, and n Ach. Therefore, age does not appear to be a confounding variable. These data may be confounded with length of managerial experience. One might argue that achieving the kinds of managerial experience that these executives achieved is a measure of managerial effectiveness in itself. A longitudinal validation study is required. It is hypothesized that a combination of n Pow and n Ach is associated with early managerial success (see Chapter 4). However, as the individual achieves higher levels of managerial success, n Ach becomes less salient and n Pow dominates. This hypothesis explains why the composite managerial motivation measure did not identify the senior executives very well in this chapter.

10 The Positive Effects of Need for Power on Job Stress and Stress Related Symptoms for Managers

STRESS AND POWER

McClelland (1979a); McClelland and Jemmott (1980); McClelland, Floor, Davidson, and Saron (1980); and McClelland, Alexander, and Marks (1982) proposed that n Pow, especially if inhibited, is related to increased physical illness. McClelland, Floor, Davidson, and Saron suggested that the mechanism for this effect is that the ". . . inhibited and/or stressed power-motive syndrome may be associated with some illnesses because it leads to chronic sympathetic activation that releases hormones (e.g., epinephrine, cortisol) that impair immune function and make the organism more susceptible to disease" (1980, p. 61). They also found that high stress was related to higher severity of illness scores. Stress has also been identified as a factor in a wide variety of other consequences, such as coronary heart disease, ulcers, stroke, backache, headache, cancer, and diabetes mellitus (Quick and Quick 1984).

Another physiological consequence of n Pow found by McClelland (1979a) is that high n Pow, when inhibited, is associated with higher blood pressure. Inhibited n Pow creates a stress condition. McClelland's results are consistent with other stress studies that have

This chapter was coauthored by Michael J. Stahl, William H. Hendrix, and Jay Coleman, all of Clemson University.

found stress to be related to increased blood pressure (Hamburg et al. 1982; Quick and Quick 1984; Weiner 1970). It is one of the typical reactions to the stress-induced "fight or flight" syndrome. Cholesterol and stress have been indicated as major factors in the development of coronary heart disease (Russek 1965). There is some indication that stress actually causes an increase in serum cholesterol and therefore increases the risk of developing coronary heart disease (Friedman et al. 1957).

This chapter is an extension of McClelland's research suggesting that inhibited n Pow affects the immune system and increases risk of disease. By using inhibited n Pow, McClelland had created a stress condition. The focus of the present research was to investigate the effect of n Pow on stress without inducing stress through inhibited n Pow. Hendrix and Stahl (1984) found that n Pow, even when not inhibited, is related to increased blood pressure level. Those results suggest that being a high n Pow individual stimulates sympathetic activity similar to that found in a stress reaction.

There are two methodological issues in much of the cited research by McClelland et al. on n Pow, stress, and illness. First, much of that research was performed by using the TAT measure of n Pow with its myriad psychometric problems (Clarke 1972; Entwisle 1972; Fineman 1977). The study by Hendrix and Stahl (1984) used an unvalidated Likert type scale of n Pow. Second, few attempts used subjects in jobs in which n Pow was necessary to be effective, such as is required for managers. Indeed, McClelland, Floor, Davidson, and Saron (1980) used subjects who were almost totally powerless, prisoners. The present research overcomes those two methodological issues by using the JCE measure of n Pow and by testing the relationship of n Pow to stress between subjects with and without power, managers and nonmanagers. It is hypothesized that n Pow is negatively correlated with job stress and related symptoms for managers, but not for nonmanagers.

METHOD

Subjects

Participants in the research study were 78 Department of Defense civilian employees working in a health care administration or accounting organization in the West. The sample was composed of 18 managers (8 males and 10 females) and 60 nonmanagers (15 males and 45 females). The managers' mean age was 43.8 years (range = 26 to 71 years) and the nonmanagers' mean age was 43.3 years (range = 20 to 64 years). The correlations of age with the JCE scores of n Pow, n Aff, and n Ach are reported in the "Results" section.

Measures

Job stress and related symptoms were measured separately in a self-report health assessment survey. Job stress was measured by three items (α = .71) that measured how stressful participants perceived their job to be overall. Commuting stress consisted of a single index of the number of miles traveled to work plus the time required to reach the work location. Physical stressors were measured by three items (α = .69). Physical stressors included measurement of the extent that the work area was noisy, too hot or too cold, and had lighting that was too bright or not bright enough. Emotional exhaustion was operationalized by nine items (α = .88) of the Maslach Burnout Inventory frequency scale (Maslach and Jackson 1981). Somatic symptoms were measured by a four item scale (α = 89) that measured the extent to which one had headaches, insomnia, and fatigue. The anxiety scale consisted of four items (α = .91) measuring the extent to which one experienced feelings of being tense, jittery, and nervous.

Procedure

Measures were collected by using a health assessment survey and the JCE during a one day health promotion seminar. Participants were informed that participation was voluntary and that they would receive feedback on their survey results by means of a computer printout containing a special identifier number known only to them. In addition, a booklet containing norms for each survey factor and an explanation of the research results was provided to each participant.

RESULTS

Table 10.1 contains the zero-order correlations broken out by managers and nonmanagers for the variables under investigation. N Pow was negatively correlated ($r = -.73$, $p < .001$) with job stress for managers. It was also negatively correlated with the other five stress related symptoms for managers. The higher the n Pow score, the better off the manager. However, none of these relationships were found for nonmanagers. Power was unrelated to stress and to the other stress related symptoms for them.

TABLE 10.1. Correlations of n Pow with Stress and Related Symptoms

	n Pow	
Stress and Symptoms	Managers (n = 18)	Nonmanagers (n = 60)
Job stress	$-.73***$	.03
Commuting stress	$-.55**$	$-.04$
Physical stressors	$-.54**$	$-.24$
Emotional exhaustion	$-.56**$	$-.15$
Somatic symptoms	$-.52*$	$-.12$
Anxiety	$-.53*$	$-.03$

$*p < .05$, one tailed.
$**p < .01$, one tailed.
$***p < .001$, one tailed.
Source: Data provided by authors.

The correlations of age with n Aff, n Pow, and n Ach for the 18 managers were not significant ($-.02$, $.26$, and $.14$, respectively). The similar correlations for the nonmanagers also were not significant ($-.13$, $-.07$, and $-.13$).

DISCUSSION AND CONCLUSION

McClelland suggested that inhibited n Pow effects a stresss response that might increase illness. He suggested that this could involve chronic sympathetic activation, which would release adrenal hormones that decrease the immune system's capacity to fight disease. Hendrix and Stahl's (1984) research suggested that high n Pow, even when not inhibited, tends to result in higher blood pressure. One possible explanation for those results is that scoring high in n Pow results in higher sympathetic activation, which affects blood pressure. This is analogous to the effect seen for Type A individuals, who have higher stress and blood pressure than Type B individuals. The present research focused on the power–job stress relationship and the effect of n Pow when not inhibited. It is possible that by using inhibited n Pow, McClelland had created a stress condition.

A proposed hypothesis was that scoring high on n Pow was beneficial for managers, in that it is a characteristic of successful managers (see Chapters 3–9). Therefore, managers scoring high on n Pow should experience less stress than those scoring low on n Pow. The relationship was not expected for nonmanagers.

The data suggest that it is desirable for managers to score higher in n Pow, since high n Pow managers experience less job related stress. This relationship was not significant for nonmanagers. The pattern of higher n Pow–lower job stress for managers than nonmanagers apparently facilitates managerial effectiveness. Managers scoring lower in n Pow experienced higher stress as they tried to cope with the managerial role. Such a pattern is associated with lower managerial effectiveness (see Chapters 3–9). Therefore, this research demonstrates the need for investigating managerial and nonmanagerial personnel separately in n Pow–stress research, which was not done by Hendrix and Stahl (1984) or by McClelland, Floor, Davidson, and Saron (1980).

Part III
Other Occupations and International Aspects

11 Ministers and Nurses: Affiliation and Power in the Helping Professions

AFFILIATION

The chapters in Part II of this book focus primarily on n Ach and n Pow. The importance of both motives for low and middle level managers was noted in Chapters 4-7. Chapters 8-10 focus on n Pow. The only explicit treatment of n Aff is in Chapter 9, concerning executives, where a combination of high n Pow and low n Aff is discussed. This chapter focuses specifically on n Aff by presenting some data on helping professions where n Aff may be functional. Supervisory, staff, and student nurses, as well as ministers, are examined.

In the motivational literature, n Aff has received the least attention of the three motives treated by McClelland. Decharms (1957), Schachter (1959), McClelland and Burnham (1976), and McClelland and Boyatzis (1982) are notable exceptions.

Schachter (1959) noted the importance of n Aff in development and maturation processes. As an individual matures and develops independence from parents, associations and friendships with others assume growing importance. Group activities and interpersonal relationships become valued. For some, the skills of developing and maintaining interpersonal relationships, and the accompanying facility of caring for and helping others, are carried over into occupational and job choices. It would seem that the helping professions would contain people high in n Aff. The concern and caring for others, which seem to be part of jobs in the helping professions, are part of n Aff.

It must also be recognized that many in the helping professions are also professionals. They have specialized education and are dedicated to their work. Therefore, many prefer that their help and advice be taken to heart; there is a certain amount of influence or n Pow involved. For the client or patient to be helped, he or she must follow the prescribed advice/behavior of the professional.

McClelland and Burnham (1976) and McClelland and Boyatzis (1982) argued that high n Aff is not associated with effective managerial leadership; managers cannot be objective in dealing with subordinates if friendships with some are involved. In one of their most often cited articles, McClelland and Burnham (1976) stated that "good guys make bum bosses." Indeed, Chapter 9 presents data on executives concerning their high n Pow and low n Aff.

To examine these issues, data from two helping professions, nurses and ministers, are presented. To test some of the earlier results on managerial profiles within helping professions, nonsupervisory staff nurses are compared with supervisory nurses. These data are also compared with two earlier groups high in n Aff: high school seniors and blue collar workers. Since the nurse sample spanned a wide age distribution, the associations of age with the three needs are also reported.

SAMPLES

Data were gathered on 20 Methodist ministers. They were all males and lived in the Southeast. Their ages ranged from 30 to the late 40s.

Data were also gathered on 25 registered nurses. They were all women and worked at two hospitals in South Carolina. Six were supervisory nurses and the other 19 were nonsupervisory staff nurses. Their ages ranged from 21 to 61, with an average of 32.

Data were also collected from 53 student nurses at Clemson University. The students were juniors and seniors. Almost all were females.

RESULTS

For the 25 registered nurses, the correlations of age with n Aff, n Pow, and n Ach were −.11, .26, and −.15, respectively. All three correlations are not significantly different from 0.

To compare the managerial profiles of the supervisory nurses with those of the nonsupervisory staff nurses, their managerial motivation scores were computed as described in Chapter 4. Those who scored above the norm means in both n Pow and n Aff were labeled high in managerial motivation; those who scored below both norm means were low in managerial motivation; others were medium. Table 11.1 contains the managerial motivation scores of the two groups. There is a significant difference between the proportion of supervisory nurses who scored high in managerial motivation (5 of 6, or .833) and the proportion of staff nurses who scored high in managerial motivation (6 of 19, or .316) (z = 2.22, p < .05). As in the earlier chapters, the managerial motivation measure discriminates between supervisors and nonsupervisors. Henceforth, the supervisory and staff nurses are treated separately.

As shown in Table 11.2, the staff nurses' mean n Aff of .57 is significantly above the norm mean of .479 described in Chapter 3 (t = 2.20, p < .05). The supervisory nurses' mean n Pow of .41 is significantly greater than the norm mean of .314 described in Chapter 3 (t = 5.88, p < .01).

DISCUSSION AND CONCLUSION

An examination of Table 11.2 relative to some data in earlier chapters reveals some interesting findings. Both the ministers and the staff nurses yielded n Aff *and* n Pow percentiles above the mean. These are the first two nonstudent groups to display such profiles. Chapters 4 and 9 describe several managerial samples with high n Pow and low n Aff. The blue collar workers of Chapter 9 and the high school seniors of Chapter 3 have high n Aff (.62 and .56, respectively), with low n Pow (.18 and .18).

The profiles indicate that the ministers and staff nurses are characterized by concern for others, interpersonal relationships, and friendships. They are also concerned with influencing others. Their being concerned and wanting to help means that the patient or troubled church member is expected to take the advice or help of the nurse or minister. Further research with others in the helping professions will demonstrate whether this profile of high n Aff and high n Pow generalizes to other helping professions.

TABLE 11.1. Managerial Motivation of Nurses

Sample	Low	Medium	High	Total
Staff nurses	3	10	6	19
Supervisory nurses	0	1	5	6
Total	3	11	11	25

Source: Data provided by author.

TABLE 11.2. Distribution of Needs, by Sample

Needs	Ministers (n = 20)	Supervisory Nurses (n = 6)	Staff Nurses n = 19)	Student Nurses (n = 53)
Aff				
M	.55	.43	.57	.46
SD	.28	.20	.18	.30
Aff percentile				
M	61	43	63	47
SD	29	25	23	29
Pow				
M	.36	.41	.32	.34
SD	.25	.04	.25	.22
Pow percentile				
M	56	63	51	54
SD	27	05	26	24
Ach				
M	.38	.61	.46	.51
SD	.33	.24	.22	.23
Ach percentile				
M	37	71	49	57
SD	30	28	26	27

Note: M = mean; SD = standard deviation.
Source: Data provided by author.

Since the helping professional deals one on one with a client in most cases, there is not as much concern for objectivity as with managers. Indeed, the data on supervisory nurses and staff nurses indicate that supervisory nurses score lower on n Aff than the staff nurses. Perhaps the supervisory nurses are more concerned with objectivity in their supervisory role.

The data in this chapter indicate that n Aff is functional in some occupations. Although the data on managers and executives presented in earlier chapters indicate that high n Aff is not functional for those groups, the present data indicate that n Aff is functional for helping professions. Combined with the results of Dalton and Todor (1979), in which n Aff was associated with effectiveness for union stewards, there are some occupational selection implications of high n Aff.

There were four student nurses in this sample whose n Aff scores were negative. Their n Aff percentile scores were 1 percent, 1 percent, 1 percent, and 3 percent. There were no staff or supervisory nurses with negative n Aff scores. The lowest n Aff percentile for a supervisory nurse was 9 percent. The lowest for a staff nurse was 10 percent. One wonders if the four student nurses with the negative n Aff scores, which means they prefer to avoid jobs with friendly relationships, would be well advised not to pursue nursing as an occupation.

12 Football Player Performance and Need for Achievement

FOOTBALL PERFORMANCE

A few published studies have been performed that explored football player performance. In general, the studies can be grouped in the two categories of physical attributes and psychological profiles. Physical attribute studies attempt to link specific physical characteristics, such as height, weight, and running speed, to football performance. Manolis (1955), Miles (1931), and McDavid (1977) are some examples. The studies had mixed results, perhaps because they did not consider a motivational component.

Some of the psychological profile studies show promise. Kroll and Petersen (1965) found that some of the Cattell Sixteen Personality Factor Questionnaire (16PF) traits were associated with successful football teams. Werner and Gottheil (1955) found that the personality of football players was stable over the four year period that they played collegiate football. Teevan and Yalof (1980) found that football starters and nonstarters exhibited a small but significant difference in n Ach. However, they used the TAT measure of n Ach, with its multiple psychometric problems (see Chapter 1).

Encouraged by the Teevan and Yalof (1980) study and knowledge of the characteristics of n Ach (see Chapter 1), it was decided to

The assistance of George Dostal of the Atlanta Falcons and of Chet Zalesky of the University of South Carolina in collecting the data is appreciated.

study the relationship of n Ach to collegiate football player performance by using the JCE. Since the person high in n Ach is characterized by displays of great individual effort to accomplish individual goals, it was hypothesized that those football players high in n Ach were higher performers.

METHOD

The Sample

The JCE was given to 56 collegiate football players at a Southeastern university. The players were all in their second, third, or fourth year. They completed the JCE after strength training sessions in the spring and summer, with the assistance of the strength training staff.

Measures

A problem with studying football player performance is a question of the measures of performance. The measures that most read about in the newspapers, such as win/lose or points scored, are really team measures. Individual measures, such as number of passes completed, number of yards rushing, or number of tackles, are not standard across all players. A few measures were found that were standard across players. Whether the player started last fall is a standard measure across players. It was a self-report measure. Like the Teevan and Yalof (1980) study, the measure assumes that the starters are higher performers than the nonstarters. Some performance measures in strength training are also standardized across individuals. Power quotients developed by B. Hoffman (1980) were used to block on the physical size of the individual from his final strength totals. These power quotients allow comparison of various physiques in terms of absolute strength. The power quotients were routinely used by the strength training coach to measure improvements. The strength training coach supervised all major lifts used in computation of the power quotients. He provided those data for this study. Three separate power quotients were used: Power Quotient Bench Press, Power Quotient Leg, and Power Quotient Total.

RESULTS

An unanticipated problem occurred in the completion of the JCE by the football players. Nine of the 56 yielded insignificant regression models. Some of the nine delivered random decisions, some circled the same number throughout the entire exercise, and some wrote that they had no idea how to follow the instructions. There are many rumors on college campuses about the reading levels of football players. The finding that 16 percent of this sample of football players could not complete the JCE in a meaningful way, compared with the typical percentage of random JCE regressions in a sample of 1–2 percent (see Chapter 3) indicates that the football players' reading levels may leave something to be desired. The analyses with power quotients and starter/nonstarter status are performed with the 47 football players who had significant JCE scores.

Table 12.1 contains the means tests between the starters and nonstarters. There is a significant, although not very strong, difference between the starters and nonstarters on n Ach. No differences were observed between the starters and nonstarters on either n Pow or n Aff.

Table 12.2 contains the correlations between n Ach and the three power quotients. Based on comments from the strength training coach that the younger football players seemed to put more effort into training than older ones, separate analyses were performed by year. Complete power quotients were obtained on 42 of the athletes. For the sophomores, there is a definite positive association between n Ach and performance in strength training using all three power quotients. For the juniors and seniors, there is no significant association.

TABLE 12.1. Mean Tests Between Starters and Nonstarters

Need	Starters (n = 7)	Nonstarters (n = 40)	t
n Aff	0.45	0.47	-0.26
n Pow	0.42	0.38	0.39
n Ach	0.61	0.49	1.44*

*p < .08, one tailed.
Source: Data provided by author.

TABLE 12.2. Correlations Between N Ach and Power Quotients, by Year

N Ach	PQB	PQL	PQT
Second year (n = 20)	.59**	.66**	.69**
Third year (n = 9)	-.01	-.25	-.34
Fourth year (n = 13)	.18	.23	.21

PQB = Power Quotient Bench.
PQL = Power Quotient Leg.
PQT = Power Quotient Total.
**p < .01, one tailed.
Source: Data provided by author.

SUMMARY AND CONCLUSION

An unanticipated finding of this research was that 16 percent of the football players were not able to complete the JCE with significant regression scores. Typically, 1–2 percent of a sample yields non-significant JCE regressions (see Chapter 3). Given the comments of some of the football players that they did not understand the JCE, the required reading level of the JCE relative to the actual reading level of the football players may be the issue. The JCE was originally designed with at least a high school reading level in mind. Indeed, one of the original samples was high school seniors (see Chapter 3). Because of this issue, Chapter 13 documents the revision and development of a lower reading level version of the JCE.

The starters were higher in n Ach than the nonstarters. The limited sample sizes may explain why the difference was not very strong. This corresponds with the findings of Teevan and Yalof (1980).

Seventeen of the 20 sophomores had no playing time the prior year. All of the 13 seniors had five or more quarters playing time. This indicates that the low performers were off the team by their senior year. Three of the juniors had no playing time, and six had more than five quarters. This differential pattern may partly explain the results with performance in strength training. In the sophomore year, 17 of 20 (85 percent) had no playing time. They were still striving for a playing role. For those athletes, striving and n Ach were associated with performance in strength training. They apparently believed that they had a chance to play and that by working at strength training, they could improve their chance of starting. It is a classic achievement situation in which individual effort can make a difference. All the seniors had played more than five quarters the prior year. They were already performing at a high level. The results indicate that at that stage their n Ach was not put to work in strength training. The juniors were mixed. Some played and some did not. The lack of feedback from not playing might explain the nonsignificant correlation between n Ach and performance in strength training.

These results are mixed partly because of the reading level issue and partly because of the small sample sizes. To overcome these two issues, the lower reading level version of the JCE discussed in Chapter 13 should be used in a longitudinal study with large samples of football players. Then it will be known if n Ach, as measured by the JCE, can be used to select high performing football players. The potential performance improvements in a collegiate or professional football program resulting from being able to identify motivational predispositions to high football playing performance seem to make such a study a worthwhile investment.

13 Policemen and a Modified Reading Level JCE

As indicated in Chapter 12, the required reading level of the JCE may be a problem for individuals with less than a high school reading level. The collegiate football players of Chapter 12 demonstrated the reading level issue when 16 percent of them were not able to complete the JCE with meaningful scores.

A firm in the Midwest that develops selection batteries for policemen expressed an interest in the JCE in the spring of 1984. When they heard about the reading level issue identified by the football study, they became concerned. The typical educational attainment of the police candidate was a high school diploma or a general equivalency degree. The firm tested for the required reading level of the JCE with the Fleischman Reading Test, and determined that the JCE required an eleventh grade reading level. The firm and the author of this book then developed and tested a lower reading level version of the JCE with a sample of policemen. A validation with policemen job behaviors was also conducted.

———————

The assistance of David E. Christiansen (Police Consultants, Inc., 825 N. Cass Ave., Suite 210, Westmont IL 60559) in the performance of this study is gratefully acknowledged.

METHOD

The Instrument

The experimental design and the format were exactly the same as the JCE described in Chapter 3 and used in Chapters 4 through 12. Specifically, a triple replicate of a 2 x 2 x 2 x 2 experiment with six warmup jobs and two decisions per job was employed. The only changes were the separation of the answer scales from the jobs and the use of shorter words.

Since there was a possibility of collecting large amounts of data, the answer scales were put on a separate sheet with the idea of developing an optically scanned answer sheet at a later date. Table 13.1 contains a sample of one of the jobs and the associated answer scales from the separate sheet.

The guiding principle in designing this form of the JCE, referred to as JCE–B, was to use shorter words to lower the reading level. For example, "likelihood" was changed to "chance," and "relationships" was changed to "relations" (see Table 13.1). The Fleischman Reading Test was used on the new form. A sixth or seventh grade required reading level was indicated.

In addition to the JCE–B, data were gathered on four other measures from the records of the police department covering the preceding two years. Absenteeism was measured as the number of days absent from the job in the preceding two years. The mean was 11.73 and the standard deviation was 18.41. The number of suspensions over the preceding two years had a mean of 0.24 and a standard deviation of 0.61. The number of written reprimands over the preceding two years had a mean of 1.91 and a standard deviation of 2.11. The annual performance evaluation score was averaged over the preceding two years. The score is the sum of ten behaviorally anchored subscales. Two sergeants and one lieutenant separately rated the policemen and then combined their ratings onto a single form that was reviewed by a captain. With the multiple raters and the multiple behaviorally anchored subscales, the evaluation score was fairly well received by the policemen. The evaluation mean over the preceding two years was 66.59 with a standard deviation of 10.33. The scale range was from 10 to 100.

TABLE 13.1. Lower Reading Level JCE Example

In this job, the chance that most of your duties will involve:

—creating and keeping friendly relations
with others is . . . . VERY LOW (5%)

—influencing the actions and thoughts of
people is . . . . VERY LOW (5%)

—reaching difficult, but possible, goals
and later receiving detailed information
about your personal performance is . . . . VERY LOW (5%)

DECISION A. Given the degrees of the 3 areas above, how much
do you want this job?

DECISION B. If you try very hard to get this job, your odds
of being hired are: VERY HIGH (95%)

Keeping in mind how much you want this job from Decision A, and considering
your odds of being hired just given, on a scale of 0 to 10, how hard would you
try to get this job?

Decision A—Attraction
(-5)   (-4)   (-3)   (-2)   (-1)   (0)   (+1)   (+2)   (+3)   (+4)   (+5)
Very Unattractive   Very Attractive

Decision B—Effort
(0)   (1)   (2)   (3)   (4)   (5)   (6)   (7)   (8)   (9)   (10)
No Effort   Great Effort

©M. J. Stahl and A. M. Harrell, 1981.

The Sample

Data were collected from 33 deputy sheriffs within a single
county sheriff's office in the Midwest. They ranged in age from the
early 20s to 55. They all had at least 2 years of experience in the job.
None of the 33 had trouble completing this revised form of the JCE.

RESULTS

The mean JCE–B scores for the 33 policemen are contained in
Table 13.2. For expository purposes, percentiles based on the norms

TABLE 13.2. Distributions of Needs for Policemen (n = 33)

Need	M	SD
Aff	.48	.41
Aff percentile	50	40
Pow	.22	.35
Pow percentile	37	36
Ach	.33	.33
Ach percentile	30	34

M = mean; SD = standard deviation.
Source: Data provided by author.

from Chapter 3 involving 1,741 subjects in seven samples are used. The mean n Aff score is almost identical with the norm mean of 0.48 from Chapter 3. However, the mean n Ach score of .33 is less than the norm mean of .46 (t = 2.24, p < .02). The mean n Pow score of .22 is also less than the norm mean of .31 (t = 1.51, p = .07).

Table 13.3 contains the correlations of the three JCE–B scores with the criterion scores. The negative correlation between n Aff and evaluation indicates that the higher the n Aff, the lower the evaluation. The positive correlation between n Ach and the number of

TABLE 13.3. Correlations Among Needs and Policemen Job Behaviors (n = 33)

Job Behaviors	n Aff	n Pow	n Ach
Absenteeism	.28	.18	-.28
Suspensions	.16	.12	.00
Reprimands	.01	-.05	.31*
Evaluations	-.37**	.00	-.13

*p = .05, two tailed.
**p < .05, two tailed.
Source: Data provided by author.

written reprimands indicates that the higher the n Ach, the higher the number of reprimands.

SUMMARY AND CONCLUSION

Based on a difference between the required reading level of the JCE and the actual reading level of the subjects observed among football players (Chapter 12), this study developed and tested a lower reading level version of the JCE, referred to as JCE-B. This revision lowers the required reading level from eleventh grade to the sixth or seventh grade. None of the 33 policemen in this study had any problem completing the lower reading level version. It is unfortunate that this version was not in existence at the time the football players were studied.

The average n Aff score of these 33 policemen was not different from the overall norm mean for n Aff. However, both the n Pow and n Ach scores were lower. Perhaps this is not surprising. McClelland's theory (McClelland 1975b; McClelland, Atkinson, Clark, and Lowell 1976) suggests that nonsupervisory adults with at most a high school diploma who are in a service oriented job where the measures of achievement are vague would score low in n Pow and n Ach.

The positive correlation between n Ach and the number of written reprimands deserves comment. Perhaps the paramilitary environment of a police department was too stifling for the high achievers. The desire of a high need achiever to do things better and to innovate is not well accepted by rigid organizations. That may have been reflected in the higher number of reprimands for those higher in n Ach.

The negative association between n Aff and the performance evaluations is also interesting. Does the high n Aff person in a work setting yield to peer pressure on restrictive work behavior or other behavior nonfunctional for the organization? Does that restrictive or nonfunctional work behavior result in lower performance evaluation? Maybe that is why few studies have been found that report a positive effect of high n Aff in industrial settings.

The overall results of this study are encouraging. As a result of this research, a version of the JCE now exists that requires only a sixth or seventh grade reading level to complete. This lower reading level version of the JCE could be used in future studies with student athletes or blue collar workers with a limited reading level. The JCE-B was used only in this chapter.

14 International Examples: Spanish and Arabic Versions of the JCE Plus Panamanian and Indian Data

All of the data in the preceding 13 chapters of this book are from the United States. Given the international flavor of some of McClelland's research (McClelland 1975b; McClelland and Winter 1969), it was decided to collect some data on n Aff, n Pow, and n Ach with the JCE in other countries for comparative purposes. This chapter describes a Spanish language JCE with associated data on engineering and business students from the University of Panama. Those data are compared with data from similar groups in prior chapters, and with data on engineering students from the Indian Institute of Technology (New Delhi). Finally, an Arabic language JCE is presented.

THE SPANISH JCE

Measure

A student pursuing a graduate degree in psychology at the University of Panama, Maria Eugenia Fonseca Mora, asked to use the

The assistance of Maria Eugenia Fonseca Mora of the University of Panama for the Spanish version, of Mahmoud Yasin of Clemson University for the Arabic version, and of Anil Gulati of Clemson University for the Indian data is appreciated.

TABLE 14.1. Spanish JCE Example

EMPLEO 2 En este empleo, la probabilidad de que la mayor parte de sus funciones involucren:

—establecer y mantener relaciones amistosas
con otros es . . . . MUY BAJA (5%)

—influir en las actividades o pensamientos
de otros individuos es . . . . MUY BAJA (5%)

—lograr metas dificiles (pero alcanzables)
y recibir despues informacion detallada
acerca de su desempeno personal es . . . . MUY BAJA (5%)

DECISION A. Teniendo en consideracion los factores antes mencionados y su probabilidad de ocurrencia, indique el atractivo de este empleo para usted.

-5	-4	-3	-2	-1	0	+1	+2	+3	+4	+5

Muy   Muy
Poco Atractivo   Atractivo

INFORMACION ADICIONAL SOBRE EL EMPLEO 2. Si usted realizara un gran esfuerzo para conseguir este empleo, la probabilidad de exito es MUY ALTA (95%).

DECISION B. Considerando el atractivo del empleo y la informacion adicional, indique cuanto esfuerzo realizaria para conseguirlo.

0	1	2	3	4	5	6	7	8	9	10

Ningun esfuerzo   Gran esfuerzo
para conseguirlo   para conseguirlo

JCE for her master's thesis (Mora 1984). The permission was given with the understanding that she would translate the JCE into Spanish, that the original copyright would be maintained, and that the resulting data would be made available to the author of this book. Table 14.1 contains a sample of the translation. As can be seen, the format is identical to the JCE described in Chapter 3 and used in Chapters 4 through 12. The experimental design is identical to that described in Chapter 3. The only difference is in language. The most literal translation possible was sought.

Sample

This Spanish version of the JCE was given to two groups of undergraduates at the University of Panama in early 1984. Thirty-nine students in their last year of studies in electrical engineering completed the JCE. Four of these students were women. All of these engineering students completed the JCE with a significant R^2. The average R^2 was .70. Fifty-one students in their last year of studies in business administration also completed the JCE. Eight of those business students had nonsignificant R^2s on their JCE scores. Consequently, they were deleted from further analysis. It is not known why such a high percentage of business students had trouble with the JCE. The average R^2 for the remaining 43 students was .72. There were 24 males and 19 females in this group of business students.

Results

A test was performed to determine if there were differences between the sexes on the three needs among the business students. Table 14.2 contains those data. As can be seen, there is no evidence of significant differences between the sexes on the three needs. The interesting feature of the table is the high level of n Ach in both sexes. This may be partly responsible for their decision to major in business.

The next test was to compare the 39 engineering students and the 43 business students with comparable students from the United

TABLE 14.2. Sex Difference Tests Among Panamanian Business Students

| Need | Men (n = 24) | | Women (n = 19) | | |
	M	SD	M	SD	t
n Aff	.45	.17	.40	.21	0.87
n Pow	.32	.24	.25	.30	0.85
n Ach	.56	.21	.56	.17	0.00

M = mean; SD = standard deviation.
Source: Data provided by author.

States. Fifty junior engineering majors and 131 junior and senior management majors in a business school in the United States are described in Chapter 6. Those data are in Table 14.3 with the Panamanian data.

TABLE 14.3. Mean Needs of Panamanian and U.S. Engineering and Business Students

| | Panamanian | | U.S. | |
| | Business (n = 43) | Engineering (n = 39) | Business (n = 131) | Engineering (n = 50) |
Needs				
n Aff	.43	.37	.55	.52
n Pow	.29	.22	.31	.30
n Ach	.56	.50	.45	.39

Source: Data provided by author.

Based on the data in Table 14.3, there are some noteworthy findings. The U.S. students scored higher in n Aff than their Panamanian counterparts in both disciplines (business students, .55 vs. .43, $t = 2.77$, $p < .01$; engineering students, .52 vs. .37, $t = 2.91$, $p < .02$; no significant differences on n Pow). The U.S. business and engineering students were lower in n Ach than the Panamanian students (business students, .45 vs. .56, $t = 2.56$, $p < .01$; engineering students, .39 vs. .50, $t = 1.81$, $p < .05$).

To test these findings in a different culture, data were gathered on 38 undergraduate engineering students at the Indian Institute of Technology (New Delhi). The English version of the JCE described and used in Chapters 3–12 was used. None of the Indian students had trouble completing it. Those data are contained in Table 14.4. A comparison of Tables 14.3 and 14.4 indicates that the Indian engineering students are similar to the Panamanian engineering students, and are different from the U.S. engineering students in the same ways that the Panamanian students differ. The Indian engineering students scored lower in n Aff than the U.S. engineering students (.37 vs. .52, $t = 2.38$, $p = .01$) and higher in n Ach (.51 vs. .39, $t = 2.04$, $p < .05$). There was no difference in n Pow scores between the Indian and the U.S. engineering students. These differences between Indian and U.S.

TABLE 14.4. Distributions of Needs for 38 Indian Engineering Students

Need	Mean	Standard Deviation
n Aff	.37	.35
n Pow	.29	.28
n Ach	.51	.29

Source: Data provided by author.

engineering students on n Aff and n Ach are identical to the results on the Panamanian students.

THE ARABIC JCE

As this book was in type, Mahmoud Yasin, a doctoral student at Clemson University, was performing his dissertation research on Arabic and American cultural differences concerning managerial and technical motivation. That research effort involves an Arabic language version of the JCE, a sample of which is in Table 14.5. The experimental design is the same as in the English and Spanish language versions of the JCE. Only the language differs. Since the data and results were not ready when this book went to press, none of those data are reported here.

CONCLUSION

This chapter presents some international examples. Based on a Spanish language and an Arabic language version of the JCE, it is now possible to collect n Aff, n Pow, and n Ach scores in a number of different countries. Yasin's dissertation should shed light on managerial and technical motivation in Arabic cultures.

The finding of no difference between men and women on the three needs among the Panamanian students corresponds to similar findings of no sex difference reported in Chapters 3 and 5. Equality between the sexes seems to include work related motivations among professionally oriented individuals.

TABLE 14.5. Arabic JCE Example

الوظيفـــــة : في هذه الوظيفة كز، كبير من المهمات المولاه اليك تحتوي علـــــى :-

  – البناء والمحافظة على علاقات جيدة مع الآخرين .... كثير الأهمية (٩٥٪)

  – التأثير على أعمال وأفكار عدد من الأفراد .... قليل الأهمية (٥٪)

  – انجاز مهمات صعبة ولكن ممكنة ثم الحصول على تقريـــــر

  – مفصل عن انجازك الشخصي .... كثير الأهمية (٩٥٪)

القرار أ : مع بقاء النقاط والنسب المئوية المذكورة أعلاه في ذهنك ،ما هي أهميــــة هذه الوظيفة بالنسبة اليـــك ؟

     ٥   ٤   ٣   ٢   ١   ٠   ١-   ٢-   ٣-   ٤-   ٥-

كثير الأهميـة   قليل الأهمية

معلومات اضافية عن الوظيفة : اذا بذلت جهدا كبيرا للحصول على هذه الوظيفة ،فاحتماليـــة الحصول عليها متوسـط (٥٠٪) .

القرار ب : مع بقاء النقاط والنسب المئوية المذكورة أعلاه بالاضافة للمعلومات الاضافية في ذهنك ، ما هو مستوى المجهود الذى ستبذله للحصول على هذه الوظيفة ؟

   ١٠   ٩   ٨   ٧   ٦   ٥   ٤   ٣   ٢   ١   ٠

أعلى مجهـــود   لا مجهـــود
مبذول   مبذول

خلال اتخاذك القرارات يجب أن تبقى في ذهنك خصائص المعلومات التي قدمت اليك . اذا كانت احتمالية وقوع حدث ما عالية جدا (٩٥٪) هذا الحــدث يحصل حوالي ٩٥ من أصل ١٠٠ محاولة مماثلة . اذا كانت احتمالية وقوع حدث ما متوسط (٥٠٪) هذا الحدث يحصل حوالي ٥٠ من أصل ١٠٠ محاولة مماثلـــة اذا كانت احتمالية وقوع حدث ما منخفض جدا (٥٠) هذا الحدث يحصل حوالـي ٥ من أصل ١٠٠ محاولة مماثلـــة .

في كل صرف ،خذ بعين الاعتبار المعلومات المتوفرة لك قبل وصولك الى القرار عن أهمية الوظيفة التي تسأل عنها بالنسبة لك . أرسم دائرة حول اختيارك من الارقام التي تلي"القرار أ " . تذكر بأنه لا يوجد هناك اختيار صحـح أو خطأ ، لذا اختر ما يناسب شعورك الشخصـــي .

بعد تعيين أختيارك -تحــــت القرار ، أدرس المعلومات المقدمة لك تحت عنوان

تابع الوظيفـــة : " معلومات اضافية " – المعلومات عن احتمالية نجاحك اذا بذلت مجهودا كبيرا لتحصيل على وظيفة ما ستقدم هنا . ارسم دائـــرة حول الرقم تحت القرار ب الذى يقع عليه اختيارك .

يجب أن تبدأ ،بأخذ القرارات الآن . ابتدأ،ا من الوظيفة رقـــم ١ الرجاء عدم نسيان اتخاذ قرار لأية وظيفة في التمرين . يجب أن تأخـذ قرار لجميع الوظائف المقدمة لك،مرة أخرى تذكرك بأنه هناك اختيــار صحيح أو خاطئ في هذا التمرين . فعبر عن مشاعرك ونواياك الحقيقـــة أجب بهدوء وبدون تسرع ، الرجاء حل التمرين في جلسة واحدة . ونعلمـك بـــأن المعلومات التي ستقدمها ستكون سرية للغايـــة .

©M. J. Stahl and A. M. Harrell, 1981.

The finding of a higher n Aff and lower n Ach among U.S. students relative to both the Panamanian and the Indian students warrants discussion. Maybe the foreign students are more dedicated to their college studies and career plans. Their higher n Ach should help them to achieve. Perhaps some of the U.S. students are "soft suburbanites" who do not need to achieve. Maybe there are other cross cultural motivational differences in n Aff and n Ach independent of performance. There might be different selection/admission policies at the various universities. Further research is needed before more definitive conclusions can be offered on these cross cultural differences.

Part IV
Conclusion

15 Summary, Applications, and the Future

Chapter 1 states the objectives of developing a new approach to the measurement of n Aff, n Pow, and n Ach; validating the new approach; and reporting on use of the approach in organizational settings. There is a need for a sound measurement approach to the three needs because of the unsatisfactory reliability and validity of the frequently used measurement approach, the TAT (Clarke 1972; Entwisle 1972; Fineman 1977).

Following the suggestions of P. J. Hoffman (1960), Mitchell and Beach (1977), and Zedeck (1977) that the behavioral decision theory modeling approach be used to study motivation, a decision modeling approach was developed. An advantage of such an approach is that scores are based on the decision-making behavior of subjects rather than on subjects' self-reports of their motivation. A decision-making exercise was designed that used a rigorous experimental design (a triple replicate of a 2 x 2 x 2 full factorial) and regression analysis of each subject's decisions (Chapters 2 and 3). An advantage of such a scoring approach is that a test for a nonsignificant regression equation highlights inconsistent data. The ensuing sections summarize the reliability and validity data of the measure, the JCE.

RELIABILITY

Test-Retest

Chapters 3 and 6 report test-retest reliabilities for n Aff, n Pow, and n Ach for four different samples. The average test-retest reliability for n Aff for those samples is .84, for n Pow is .82, and for n Ach is .81. Chapter 6 reports on test-retest reliability coefficients for the composite managerial motivation measure for two samples. The average test-retest reliability coefficient is .70. Such reliability coefficients are substantially higher than reliability coefficients averaging approximately .30 reported by Entwisle (1972) and Fineman (1977) in two comprehensive reviews of the TAT.

Internal Consistency

An advantage of this measurement approach is that a check on the internal consistency of each subject is performed. A nonsignificant regression equation indicates internally inconsistent data from a respondent. Typically, 1 or 2 percent of a sample yields nonsignificant regression equations, as noted by R^2s less than .315. An exception is in Chapter 12, where 16 percent of the football players yielded nonsignificant regression equations. This was probably due to the required reading level of the JCE relative to their actual reading level. This led to the development of a lower reading level version of the JCE, JCE–B, which was developed and tested with policemen (see Chapter 13). Chapters 3–12 and 14 are based on the JCE whose development is reported on in Chapter 3. Chapter 3 reports an average R^2 of .77 across seven samples involving 1,741 subjects. Such an internal consistency index is typical for the JCE and speaks well of its psychometric qualities.

VALIDITY

Several different types of validity tests, including construct validity, convergent-discriminant validity, and criterion related validity (both concurrent and predictive), were performed on many separate samples. McClelland's theory, which is the basis for many of the tests, is reviewed in Chapter 1.

Construct Validity

In their classic paper on construct validity, Cronbach and Meehl (1955) mentioned that one way to examine construct validity is to test for differences on the constructs among groups that were hypothesized to differ in ways specified by the theory. Several chapters tested differences among groups. All percentiles used in this book are based on the norms across seven samples involving 1,741 subjects in Chapter 3. The following group difference tests correspond to the theory and lend support to the construct validity of the JCE.

Affiliation

Senior executives (Chapter 9) were found to be the lowest scoring group in n Aff among all the samples in this book, with an average n Aff percentile of 15 percent. Blue collar workers (Chapter 9), ministers, and nonsupervisory nurses (Chapter 11) were among the highest in n Aff, with average percentiles of 70 percent, 61 percent, and 63 percent, respectively.

Power

The senior executives and the Air Force colonels at the Air War College (Chapter 9) were the highest in n Pow, with average n Pow percentiles of 85 percent, and 82 percent, respectively. The lowest scoring groups in terms of n Pow were high school seniors (Chapter 3), blue collar workers (Chapter 9), engineers and computer scientists (Chapter 8), policemen (Chapter 13), and Panamanian engineering students (Chapter 14), with average n Pow percentiles of 32 percent, 32 percent, 37 percent, 36 percent, 37 percent, and 37 percent, respectively.

Achievement

The highest scoring groups in n Ach were two groups of scientists and engineers (Chapter 8) and officer graduate students (Chapter 3), with average n Ach percentiles of 73 percent. The lowest scoring were the student senators of Chapter 6, at 21 percent, followed by the policemen at 30 percent.

Managerial Motivation

A group of supervisors in Chapter 4 scored highest on the managerial motivation measure: 10 of 10 scored high on the composite measure. A group of supervisory nurses (Chapter 11) had the second highest percent in the high managerial motivation category, with five of six in the high category. The sample with the lowest percent in the high managerial category was a group of 50 student engineers in Chapter 6, who only had 16 percent scoring high in managerial motivation, followed by the blue collar workers of Chapter 4, who placed 25 percent in the high managerial motivation category. These group difference tests support the construct validity of the composite managerial motivation measure, particularly for low level managers.

Convergent-Discriminant Validity

One convergent-discriminant validity study was performed. Chapter 3 contains correlations between the JCE and the Steers and Braunstein (1976) Manifest Needs Questionnaire. The hypothesized pattern of correlations emerged. The like needs, as measured by both instruments, converged. Specifically, JCE n Aff, n Pow, and n Ach were significantly associated with the three respective needs on the questionnaire. The unlike needs, as measured by the two different instruments, diverged.

Concurrent Validity

Affiliation

Two concurrent validity tests for n Aff are reported in two separate chapters. Chapter 3 reports a significant correlation between the number of hours spent with friends and n Aff for undergraduates ($r = .22$). Chapter 13 reports a significant negative correlation between n Aff and performance evaluations of policemen ($r = -.37$). These two concurrent validity coefficients indicate that although high n Aff may lead to deeper friendships, it may also lead to poorer job performance if it is a substitute for work related needs like n Ach or n Pow. Maybe this is why McClelland's literature reveals few positive outcomes of n Aff in organizational settings.

Power

Several concurrent validity tests are reported in various chapters. Chapter 2 reports a significant, positive association between Air Force officer performance appraisal scores and n Pow (r = .38). Chapter 3 reports significant, positive associations between n Pow and high school leadership activity for a nationwide sample of 1,450 Air Force Academy cadets (r = .05), and between n Pow and the number of people supervised for 28 supervisors (r = .28). College students who held a campus student office scored significantly higher in n Pow than those who did not hold an office. Managerial performance appraisal scores were significantly related to n Pow (r = .36) in Chapter 8. Chapter 10 reports significant, negative associations between n Pow and job stress (r = -.73), commuting stress (r = -.55), physical stressors (r = -.54), emotional exhaustion (r = -.56), somatic symptoms (r = -.52), and anxiety (r = -.53) for 18 managers. However, none of those associations between n Pow and stress were significant for 60 nonmanagers in the same study. N Pow is positively related to leadership activity and managerial performance. Higher n Pow also appears to be beneficial for managers because it is associated with lower stress.

Achievement

N Ach is significantly related to individual performance in several chapters. Chapter 2 notes a significant, positive association between n Ach and graduate grade point average for 156 graduate students (r = .20). Of 173 scientists and engineers, those who had published in the previous year scored significantly higher in n Ach than those who had not. Chapter 3 reports three positive associations between n Ach and individual performance. A significant, positive association is reported between n Ach and high school academic record (r = .06) for 1,450 Air Force Academy cadets. A significant, positive correlation between n Ach and the number of hours spent studying (r = .23) is reported for 74 management undergraduates. A significant association between n Ach and academic grade point average (r = .26) is noted for 45 accounting undergraduates and for 1,450 Air Force Academy cadets after one year (r = .12). Chapter 12 reports two positive findings for n Ach and football players. Football players who were on the starting team scored significantly higher in n Ach than those who did not start. There are also significant, positive associations between n Ach and three different measures of performance in strength training. Chapter 13 reports a significant, positive association between n Ach and the number of reprimands for 33 policemen (r = .31). It appears that the high n Ach person does not fare well in the restrictive, paramilitary police environment. All the other findings indicate that n Ach is positively associated with individual performance.

Managerial Motivation

Chapter 4 reports some concurrent validity findings for the composite managerial motivation measure, which is a combination of n Ach and n Pow. Those who scored above the overall mean on both n Ach and n Pow were labeled high in managerial motivation; those who scored low on both needs were labeled low in managerial motivation; others were labeled medium. This fusing of high n Ach and high n Pow into high managerial motivation is theoretically developed in Chapter 4. Significant, positive associations between managerial motivation and status as a supervisor or not a supervisor among 10 supervisors and 24 nonsupervisors within an organization (r = .85); between managerial motivation and managerial performance scores for 24 managers within a firm (r = .36); and between managerial motivation and managerial promotion for 50 managers in one firm (r = .50) are reported. Indeed, managerial motivation is associated with managerially relevant behaviors for low and mid level managers.

Predictive Validity

One longitudinal study with a large, nationwide sample is reported in this book. Chapter 5 reports the results of a two year longitudinal study in which the JCE was administered to the entire entering freshman class at the Air Force Academy (n > 1,400). Two year turnover data, two year cumulative military performance data, and two year cumulative academic performance data were compared with the cadets' managerial motivation scores. Since the cadets were in training to assume leadership roles in the military as officers, the comparison with turnover data is of particular interest. Data analysis demonstrated that those cadets who scored high in managerial motivation had significantly lower turnover rates, higher military performance averages, and higher academic performance averages than those who scored low in managerial motivation. The combination of high n Ach and high n Pow in the high managerial motivation score yielded all three beneficial longitudinal results for those in the nationwide sample who were being trained for leadership roles.

Biases

Social Desirability Bias

Two different social desirability tests were performed. Chapter 3 reports nonsignificant correlations between JCE n Aff, n Pow, and n Ach, and the Crowne-Marlowe (1960) Social Desirability Index for 74 undergraduates. Chapter 7 reports nonsignificant correlations between JCE n Aff, n Pow, n Ach, managerial motivation, and the social desirability index. The absence of a social desirability bias indicates that the JCE has overcome a bias typically associated with self-report measures of motivation.

Sex Bias

Chapters 3 and 14 report no significant differences between the sexes on n Aff, n Pow, and n Ach for four different samples. Nor was there a difference between the sexes on managerial motivation scores in Chapters 5 and 7.

Minority Bias

Chapter 5 reports no significant relationship between minority status and managerial motivation scores for a nationwide sample of 1,400 Air Force Academy cadets.

Age Bias

Chapters 10 and 11 report nonsignificant correlations between age and n Aff, n Pow, and n Ach for samples of nurses, managers, and nonsupervisors. The absence of sex, minority, and age biases indicates that the JCE could be used in a selection mode.

PSYCHOMETRIC SUMMARY

The preceding reliability and validity data present an optimistic outlook for this decision modeling approach to n Aff, n Pow, n Ach, and managerial motivation. The reliabilities indicate substantially high levels of both internal and test-retest consistency. The criterion related validities indicate the ability to explain and predict organizationally relevant behaviors, such as academic performance, managerial performance, military performance, athletic performance, research performance, stress, and turnover. The group difference tests demonstrate the JCE's ability to identify those groups who ought to score high and low on the various needs. For example, executives and colonels scored highest on n Pow; engineers, scientists, and graduate students scored highest on n Ach; blue collar workers, nonsupervisory nurses, and ministers scored highest on n Aff; and managers and supervisory nurses scored highest on managerial motivation. No evidence of social desirability bias, sex bias, minority bias, or age bias was found in the data. The expected pattern of convergence and divergence was found with an alternative measure of the three needs. Based on the preceding, it appears that this book's objectives of developing and validating a new decision modeling approach to the measurement of n Aff, n Pow, and n Ach have been met.

The only disappointment was the required reading level of the JCE highlighted in the study of athletes (Chapter 12). Therefore, a lower reading level version, the JCE–B, was developed and tested in Chapter 13. It is meant for subjects with between a seventh and an eleventh grade reading level. The JCE used in the other chapters of this book requires at least an eleventh grade reading level. Since most of the samples for this research are college students, managers, and professional employees, and eleventh grade reading level is not an issue.

APPLICATIONS

Managerial and Executive Motivation

A combination of high n Ach and high n Pow labeled as high managerial motivation effectively identified managers from nonmanagers and was associated with managerial performance and promotion (Chapter 4). The composite managerial motivation measure was also able to predict performance and turnover in a two year study of officer cadets (Chapter 5), and to identify managerial potential at an early age among campus leaders (Chapter 6). The composite measure also discriminated between supervisory and nonsupervisory nurses (Chapter 11). Therefore, it appears that the combination of high n Pow and high n Ach in the composite managerial motivation measure can effectively be used to identify and select low and mid level managers.

There are skill bases for managerial selection, such as budgetary skills and communication skills. Many of those managerial skills are trainable. However, few motivations are trainable (Steger 1978). N Pow is especially difficult to train because it is so stable (McClelland 1981). Therefore, motivation should be a basis for selection and skill should be a basis for training.

Managers in high technology and engineering firms are differentiated from nonmanagerial professional employees primarily in terms of n Pow. Both groups are high in n Ach. Therefore, selection of managers of professional employees could be based partly on n Pow. The literature on the management of research, development, and engineering organizations is full of examples in which the most technically competent professional (high n Ach and low n Pow) is promoted to management and proves to be a failure. Such costs can be avoided if n Pow is considered.

The data on executives indicate that n Pow is definitely dominant among executives. The n Ach motive may be somewhat satisfied by the time they reach executive status. At that stage, n Aff is the lowest. In addition to potential selection implications, such executive profiles may have training implications. Low and mid level managers could be exposed to such executive profiles in managerial training. The lower level managers could then make informed decisions on whether they wished to strive for such positions.

Technical Motivation

The data on scientists and engineers in this book indicate a substantially different profile for technical motivation and performance in nonsupervisory technical jobs than the profile for managers and executives. The scientists and engineers in Chapter 2 who were high performers scored higher in n Ach than the low performers. The nonsupervisory engineers and computer scientists in Chapter 8 were among the highest scoring subjects on n Ach. They were also among the lowest scoring in n Pow. Their n Aff was also low. It appears that high n Ach could be a motivational basis for selection of scientists and engineers. The same should hold true for other nonsupervisory technical employees, such as accountants, computer system analysts, and computer programmers. Such technical, professional jobs are almost a classic definition of the application of n Ach per McClelland's theory.

Athletic Motivation

The data on performance among collegiate football players (Chapter 12) suggest that n Ach could be a motivational basis for selection of athletes. The revised lower reading level version of the JCE, the JCE–B, should yield even better results with such subjects.

Helping Professions

The ministers' and nurses' profiles in Chapter 11 indicate a unique combination of moderate to high n Pow *and* n Aff in the helping professions. Such a profile was not found elsewhere among working adults. Indeed, in the managerial role, high n Pow and n Aff lead to role conflict as the manager is torn between affiliation, with its implication of not offending the friend, and power, with its implication of influencing the individual to act. Care for the individual (n Aff) and change in behavior (n Pow) are both appropriate in the helping professions. A balance of the two needs could be a basis for selection.

FUTURE RESEARCH

In the realm of managerial motivation, it is possible that a specific organization would be better served by a linear combination of n Ach and n Pow different from that used in this book. It is also conceivable that in a specific organization, a linear combination of n Ach, n Pow, and n Aff would better model executive performance than in Chapter 9. Therefore, an organization that wished to be conservative in its personnel decision making would be advised to validate these needs in its organization prior to use of the instrument for selection (American Psychological Association 1980; Rubenfeld and Crino 1981).

More needs to be known about how the combination of n Ach and n Pow associated with managerial performance evolves to dominance of n Pow among senior executives. Although short term changes are rare, career long term evolutions are possible. Therefore, more research could be performed on effective combinations of the needs across organizational hierarchies and through careers.

More needs to be known about managerial and technical motivation in other countries. Since U.S. firms are conducting more international operations, identifying successful motivational profiles for managerial and technical positions in other countries assumes greater importance. Sending U.S. employees who fit the prevailing motivational profiles of particular countries also assumes importance. The development of the Spanish and Arabic versions of the JCE (Chapter 14) is a step in that direction. Perhaps the power of a decision modeling approach to identifying managerial and technical motivation based on n Aff, n Pow, and n Ach might be demonstrated in other countries as it has been demonstrated by this book in this country.

McClelland's theory of n Aff, n Pow, and n Ach is alive and well. This book demonstrates that a psychometrically sound instrument now exists to operationalize the theory in a number of organizational contexts.

Appendix

A JOB CHOICE
DECISION-MAKING EXERCISE

Michael J. Stahl, Ph.D.
Assessment Enterprises

A JOB CHOICE
DECISION-MAKING EXERCISE

This decision making exercise deals with hypothetical situations. In this way, it simulates the job preference and effort decisions most individuals encounter at some point in a career. As you complete the exercise, you should project yourself into a hypothetical situation. Assume you are seeking a job and you are in the process of judging a number of jobs available to you which you are qualified to fill. All of these jobs are exactly alike in the usual attributes, such as pay, benefits, etc. These jobs differ only in regards to the information presented to you about three key factors. A sample job is presented below for your advance examination before you begin the exercise.

Please notice you are asked to arrive at two decisions in relation to each of the hypothetical jobs presented to you. The first decision involves judging the attractiveness of the job (DECISION A). The second decision involves judging how much effort you would exert to get the particular job.

JOB X

In this job, the likelihood that a major portion of your duties will involve

—*establishing and maintaining friendly relationships with others is*. . . . .   VERY HIGH (95%)

—*influencing the activities or thoughts of a number of individuals is* . . . .   VERY LOW   (5%)

—*accomplishing difficult (but feasible) goals and later receiving detailed information about your personal performance is* . . . .   VERY HIGH (95%)

DECISION A. With the factors and associated likelihood levels shown above in mind, indicate the attractiveness of this job to you.

−5	−4	−3	−2	−1	0	+1	+2	+3	+4	+5

Very
Unattractive   Very
                                                                                                       Attractive

FURTHER INFORMATION ABOUT JOB X If you exert a great deal of effort to get this job, the likelihood that you will be successful is MEDIUM (50%).

DECISION B. With both the attractiveness and likelihood information presented above in mind, indicate the level of effort you would exert to get this job.

0	1	2	3	4	5	6	7	8	9	10

Zero effort   Great effort
to get it   to get it

As you arrive at your decisions, the characteristics of the information presented to you about each job should be kept in mind. If an event's likelihood is Very High (95%), then it will occur in about 95 of 100 similar situations. If an event's likelihood is Medium (50%), then it will occur in about 50 of 100 similar situations. If an event's likelihood is Very Low (5%), then it will occur in only about 5 of 100 similar situations.

In each instance, consider the information presented to you and then arrive at your judgement of the attractiveness of that particular job to **you.** Circle the number under DECISION A which indicates your choice. Remember, there are no "correct" or "incorrect" choices, so follow your **own** feelings.

After indicating your choice under DECISION A, examine the information presented as FURTHER INFORMATION. Data about the likelihood you will be successful if you exert a great deal of effort to get the particular job is presented here. Circle the number under DECISION B which indicates your choice.

You should now begin to make the actual decisions, starting with Job #1. Be careful not to skip a job; you should make decisions about each of the jobs presented to you. Once again, remember there are no "correct" or "incorrect" decisions in this exercise, so express your true feelings and intentions. You should work briskly without hurrying. Please complete the exercise in a single sitting.

© M. J. Stahl and A. M. Harrell, 1981

JOB # 1

In this job, the likelihood that a major portion of your duties will involve

—establishing and maintaining friendly relationships with others is..	VERY HIGH (95%)
—influencing the activities or thoughts of a number of individuals is	VERY HIGH (95%)
—accomplishing difficult (but feasible) goals and later receiving detailed information about your personal performance is	VERY HIGH (95%)

DECISION A. With the factors and associated likelihood levels shown above in mind, indicate the attractiveness of this job to you.

−5	−4	−3	−2	−1	0	+1	+2	+3	+4	+5
Very Unattractive										Very Attractive

FURTHER INFORMATION ABOUT JOB #1 If you exert a great deal of effort to get this job, the likelihood that you will be successful is MEDIUM (50%).

DECISION B. With both the attractiveness and likelihood information presented above in mind, indicate the level of effort you would exert to get this job.

0	1	2	3	4	5	6	7	8	9	10
Zero effort to get it										Great effort to get it

JOB # 2

In this job, the likelihood that a major portion of your duties will involve

—establishing and maintaining friendly relationships with others is..	VERY LOW (5%)
—influencing the activities or thoughts of a number of individuals is	VERY LOW (5%)
—accomplishing difficult (but feasible) goals and later receiving detailed information about your personal performance is	VERY LOW (5%)

DECISION A. With the factors and associated likelihood levels shown above in mind, indicate the attractiveness of this job to you.

−5	−4	−3	−2	−1	0	+1	+2	+3	+4	+5
Very Unattractive										Very Attractive

FURTHER INFORMATION ABOUT JOB #2 If you exert a great deal of effort to get this job, the likelihood that you will be successful is VERY HIGH (95%).

DECISION B. With both the attractiveness and likelihood information presented above in mind, indicate the level of effort you would exert to get this job.

0	1	2	3	4	5	6	7	8	9	10
Zero effort to get it										Great effort to get it

JOB # 3

In this job, the likelihood that a major portion of your duties will involve

—establishing and maintaining friendly relationships with others is... VERY LOW (5%)

—influencing the activities or thoughts of a number of individuals is .... VERY HIGH (95%)

—accomplishing difficult (but feasible) goals and later receiving detailed information about your personal performance is .... VERY LOW (5%)

DECISION A. With the factors and associated likelihood levels shown above in mind, indicate the attractiveness of this job to you.

−5   −4   −3   −2   −1   0   +1   +2   +3   +4   +5
Very   Very
Unattractive   Attractive

FURTHER INFORMATION ABOUT JOB #3 If you exert a great deal of effort to get this job, the likelihood that you will be successful is MEDIUM (50%).

DECISION B. With both the attractiveness and likelihood information presented above in mind, indicate the level of effort you would exert to get this job.

0   1   2   3   4   5   6   7   8   9   10
Zero effort   Great effort
to get it   to get it

JOB # 4

In this job, the likelihood that a major portion of your duties will involve

—establishing and maintaining friendly relationships with others is... VERY HIGH (95%)

—influencing the activities or thoughts of a number of individuals is .... VERY LOW (5%)

—accomplishing difficult (but feasible) goals and later receiving detailed information about your personal performance is .... VERY HIGH (95%)

DECISION A. With the factors and associated likelihood levels shown above in mind, indicate the attractiveness of this job to you.

−5   −4   −3   −2   −1   0   +1   +2   +3   +4   +5
Very   Very
Unattractive   Attractive

FURTHER INFORMATION ABOUT JOB #4 If you exert a great deal of effort to get this job, the likelihood that you will be successful is VERY LOW (5%).

DECISION B. With both the attractiveness and likelihood information presented above in mind, indicate the level of effort you would exert to get this job.

0   1   2   3   4   5   6   7   8   9   10
Zero effort   Great effort
to get it   to get it

JOB # 5

In this job, the likelihood that a major portion of your duties
will involve

—*establishing and maintaining friendly relationships*
  with others is... VERY LOW (5%)

—*influencing the activities or thoughts of a number*
  of individuals is .... VERY LOW (5%)

—*accomplishing difficult (but feasible) goals and*
  later receiving detailed information about your
  personal performance is .... VERY HIGH (95%)

DECISION A. With the factors and associated likelihood levels shown above
in mind, indicate the attractiveness of this job to you.

-5 -4 -3 -2 -1 0 $+1$ $+2$ $+3$ $+4$ $+5$
Very   Very
Unattractive   Attractive

FURTHER INFORMATION ABOUT JOB #5 If you exert a great deal of effort to get
this job, the likelihood that you will be successful is VERY LOW (5%).

DECISION B. With both the attractiveness and likelihood information presented
above in mind, indicate the level of effort you would exert to get this job.

0 1 2 3 4 5 6 7 8 9 10
Zero effort   Great effort
to get it   to get it

JOB # 6

In this job, the likelihood that a major portion of your duties
will involve

—*establishing and maintaining friendly relationships*
  with others is... VERY HIGH (95%)

—*influencing the activities or thoughts of a number*
  of individuals is .... VERY HIGH (95%)

—*accomplishing difficult (but feasible) goals and*
  later receiving detailed information about your
  personal performance is .... VERY LOW (5%)

DECISION A. With the factors and associated likelihood levels shown above
in mind, indicate the attractiveness of this job to you.

-5 -4 -3 -2 -1 0 $+1$ $+2$ $+3$ $+4$ $+5$
Very   Very
Unattractive   Attractive

FURTHER INFORMATION ABOUT JOB #6 If you exert a great deal of effort to
get this job, the likelihood that you will be successful is VERY HIGH (95%).

DECISION B. With both the attractiveness and likelihood information presented
above in mind, indicate the level of effort you would exert to get this job.

0 1 2 3 4 5 6 7 8 9 10
Zero effort   Great effort
to get it   to get it

© M. J. Stahl and A. M. Harrell, 1981

JOB # 7

In this job, the likelihood that a major portion of your duties will involve

—*establishing and maintaining friendly relationships with others is*.. **VERY HIGH** (95%)

—*influencing the activities or thoughts of a number of individuals is* .... **VERY LOW** (5%)

—*accomplishing difficult (but feasible) goals and later receiving detailed information about your personal performance is* .... **VERY LOW** (5%)

DECISION A. With the factors and associated likelihood levels shown above in mind, indicate the attractiveness of this job to you.

−5	−4	−3	−2	−1	0	+1	+2	+3	+4	+5

Very
Unattractive

Very
Attractive

FURTHER INFORMATION ABOUT JOB #7 If you exert a great deal of effort to get this job, the likelihood that you will be successful is VERY LOW (5%).

DECISION B. With both the attractiveness and likelihood information presented above in mind, indicate the level of effort you would exert to get this job.

0	1	2	3	4	5	6	7	8	9	10

Zero effort
to get it

Great effort
to get it

JOB # 8

In this job, the likelihood that a major portion of your duties will involve

—*establishing and maintaining friendly relationships with others is*.. **VERY LOW** (5%)

—*influencing the activities or thoughts of a number of individuals is* .... **VERY LOW** (5%)

—*accomplishing difficult (but feasible) goals and later receiving detailed information about your personal performance is* .... **VERY HIGH** (95%)

DECISION A. With the factors and associated likelihood levels shown above in mind, indicate the attractiveness of this job to you.

−5	−4	−3	−2	−1	0	+1	+2	+3	+4	+5

Very
Unattractive

Very
Attractive

FURTHER INFORMATION ABOUT JOB #8 If you exert a great deal of effort to get this job, the likelihood that you will be successful is VERY HIGH (95%).

DECISION B. With both the attractiveness and likelihood information presented above in mind, indicate the level of effort you would exert to get this job.

0	1	2	3	4	5	6	7	8	9	10

Zero effort
to get it

Great effort
to get it

JOB # 9

In this job, the likelihood that a major portion of your duties will involve

—establishing and maintaining friendly relationships with others is.................................... VERY LOW (5%)

—influencing the activities or thoughts of a number of individuals is .... VERY HIGH (95%)

—accomplishing difficult (but feasible) goals and later receiving detailed information about your personal performance is .... VERY HIGH (95%)

DECISION A. With the factors and associated likelihood levels shown above in mind, indicate the attractiveness of this job to you.

−5	−4	−3	−2	−1	0	+1	+2	+3	+4	+5

Very
Unattractive

Very
Attractive

FURTHER INFORMATION ABOUT JOB #9 If you exert a great deal of effort to get this job, the likelihood that you will be successful is MEDIUM (50%).

DECISION B. With both the attractiveness and likelihood information presented above in mind, indicate the level of effort you would exert to get this job.

0	1	2	3	4	5	6	7	8	9	10

Zero effort
to get it

Great effort
to get it

JOB # 10

In this job, the likelihood that a major portion of your duties will involve

—establishing and maintaining friendly relationships with others is.................................... VERY HIGH (95%)

—influencing the activities or thoughts of a number of individuals is .... VERY LOW (5%)

—accomplishing difficult (but feasible) goals and later receiving detailed information about your personal performance is .... VERY HIGH (95%)

DECISION A. With the factors and associated likelihood levels shown above in mind, indicate the attractiveness of this job to you.

−5	−4	−3	−2	−1	0	+1	+2	+3	+4	+5

Very
Unattractive

Very
Attractive

FURTHER INFORMATION ABOUT JOB #10 If you exert a great deal of effort to get this job, the likelihood that you will be successful is VERY LOW (5%).

DECISION B. With both the attractiveness and likelihood information presented above in mind, indicate the level of effort you would exert to get this job.

0	1	2	3	4	5	6	7	8	9	10

Zero effort
to get it

Great effort
to get it

© M. J. Stahl and A. M. Harrell, 1981

JOB # 11

In this job, the likelihood that a major portion of your duties will involve

—*establishing and maintaining friendly relationships with others is*.. **VERY HIGH (95%)**

—*influencing the activities or thoughts of a number of individuals is* .... **VERY HIGH (95%)**

—*accomplishing difficult (but feasible) goals and later receiving detailed information about your personal performance is* .... **VERY HIGH (95%)**

DECISION A. With the factors and associated likelihood levels shown above in mind, indicate the attractiveness of this job to you.

−5	−4	−3	−2	−1	0	+1	+2	+3	+4	+5

Very
Unattractive

Very
Attractive

FURTHER INFORMATION ABOUT JOB #11 If you exert a great deal of effort to get this job, the likelihood that you will be successful is VERY HIGH (95%).

DECISION B. With both the attractiveness and likelihood information presented above in mind, indicate the level of effort you would exert to get this job.

0	1	2	3	4	5	6	7	8	9	10

Zero effort
to get it

Great effort
to get it

JOB # 12

In this job, the likelihood that a major portion of your duties will involve

—*establishing and maintaining friendly relationships with others is*.. **VERY LOW (5%)**

—*influencing the activities or thoughts of a number of individuals is* .... **VERY HIGH (95%)**

—*accomplishing difficult (but feasible) goals and later receiving detailed information about your personal performance is* .... **VERY LOW (5%)**

DECISION A. With the factors and associated likelihood levels shown above in mind, indicate the attractiveness of this job to you.

−5	−4	−3	−2	−1	0	+1	+2	+3	+4	+5

Very
Unattractive

Very
Attractive

FURTHER INFORMATION ABOUT JOB #12 If you exert a great deal of effort to get this job, the likelihood that you will be successful is VERY LOW (5%).

DECISION B. With both the attractiveness and likelihood information presented above in mind, indicate the level of effort you would exert to get this job.

0	1	2	3	4	5	6	7	8	9	10

Zero effort
to get it

Great effort
to get it

© M. J. Stahl and A. M. Harrell, 1981

JOB # 13

In this job, the likelihood that a major portion of your duties will involve

—*establishing and maintaining friendly relationships with others is*.. VERY LOW (5%)

—*influencing the activities or thoughts of a number of individuals is* .... VERY LOW (5%)

—*accomplishing difficult (but feasible) goals and later receiving detailed information about your personal performance is* .... VERY LOW (5%)

DECISION A. With the factors and associated likelihood levels shown above in mind, indicate the attractiveness of this job to you.

−5	−4	−3	−2	−1	0	+1	+2	+3	+4	+5

Very
Unattractive

Very
Attractive

FURTHER INFORMATION ABOUT JOB #13 If you exert a great deal of effort to get this job, the likelihood that you will be successful is MEDIUM (50%).

DECISION B. With both the attractiveness and likelihood information presented above in mind, indicate the level of effort you would exert to get this job.

0	1	2	3	4	5	6	7	8	9	10

Zero effort
to get it

Great effort
to get it

JOB # 14

In this job, the likelihood that a major portion of your duties will involve

—*establishing and maintaining friendly relationships with others is*.. VERY HIGH (95%)

—*influencing the activities or thoughts of a number of individuals is* .... VERY HIGH (95%)

—*accomplishing difficult (but feasible) goals and later receiving detailed information about your personal performance is* .... VERY LOW (5%)

DECISION A. With the factors and associated likelihood levels shown above in mind, indicate the attractiveness of this job to you.

−5	−4	−3	−2	−1	0	+1	+2	+3	+4	+5

Very
Unattractive

Very
Attractive

FURTHER INFORMATION ABOUT JOB #14 If you exert a great deal of effort to get this job, the likelihood that you will be successful is VERY HIGH (95%).

DECISION B. With both the attractiveness and likelihood information presented above in mind, indicate the level of effort you would exert to get this job.

0	1	2	3	4	5	6	7	8	9	10

Zero effort
to get it

Great effort
to get it

JOB # 15

In this job, the likelihood that a major portion of your duties will involve

—establishing and maintaining friendly relationships with others is...	VERY LOW	(5%)
—influencing the activities or thoughts of a number of individuals is	VERY LOW	(5%)
—accomplishing difficult (but feasible) goals and later receiving detailed information about your personal performance is	VERY LOW	(5%)

DECISION A. With the factors and associated likelihood levels shown above in mind, indicate the attractiveness of this job to you.

−5	−4	−3	−2	−1	0	+1	+2	+3	+4	+5

Very
Unattractive

Very
Attractive

FURTHER INFORMATION ABOUT JOB #15 If you exert a great deal of effort to get this job, the likelihood that you will be successful is VERY HIGH (95%).

DECISION B. With both the attractiveness and likelihood information presented above in mind, indicate the level of effort you would exert to get this job.

0	1	2	3	4	5	6	7	8	9	10

Zero effort
to get it

Great effort
to get it

JOB # 16

In this job, the likelihood that a major portion of your duties will involve

—establishing and maintaining friendly relationships with others is...	VERY LOW	(5%)
—influencing the activities or thoughts of a number of individuals is	VERY HIGH	(95%)
—accomplishing difficult (but feasible) goals and later receiving detailed information about your personal performance is	VERY HIGH	(95%)

DECISION A. With the factors and associated likelihood levels shown above in mind, indicate the attractiveness of this job to you.

−5	−4	−3	−2	−1	0	+1	+2	+3	+4	+5

Very
Unattractive

Very
Attractive

FURTHER INFORMATION ABOUT JOB #16 If you exert a great deal of effort to get this job, the likelihood that you will be successful is VERY LOW (5%).

DECISION B. With both the attractiveness and likelihood information presented above in mind, indicate the level of effort you would exert to get this job.

0	1	2	3	4	5	6	7	8	9	10

Zero effort
to get it

Great effort
to get it

© M. J. Stahl and A. M. Harrell, 1981

JOB # 17

In this job, the likelihood that a major portion of your duties will involve

—establishing and maintaining friendly relationships with others is...	VERY LOW	(5%)
—influencing the activities or thoughts of a number of individuals is	VERY LOW	(5%)
—accomplishing difficult (but feasible) goals and later receiving detailed information about your personal performance is	VERY HIGH	(95%)

DECISION A. With the factors and associated likelihood levels shown above in mind, indicate the attractiveness of this job to you.

−5	−4	−3	−2	−1	0	+1	+2	+3	+4	+5

Very
Unattractive
                                                                                    Very
                                                                                    Attractive

FURTHER INFORMATION ABOUT JOB #17 If you exert a great deal of effort to get this job, the likelihood that you will be successful is MEDIUM (50%).

DECISION B. With both the attractiveness and likelihood information presented above in mind, indicate the level of effort you would exert to get this job.

0	1	2	3	4	5	6	7	8	9	10

Zero effort
to get it
                                                                                    Great effort
                                                                                    to get it

JOB # 18

In this job, the likelihood that a major portion of your duties will involve

—establishing and maintaining friendly relationships with others is...	VERY HIGH	(95%)
—influencing the activities or thoughts of a number of individuals is	VERY LOW	(5%)
—accomplishing difficult (but feasible) goals and later receiving detailed information about your personal performance is	VERY LOW	(5%)

DECISION A. With the factors and associated likelihood levels shown above in mind, indicate the attractiveness of this job to you.

−5	−4	−3	−2	−1	0	+1	+2	+3	+4	+5

Very
Unattractive
                                                                                    Very
                                                                                    Attractive

FURTHER INFORMATION ABOUT JOB #18 If you exert a great deal of effort to get this job, the likelihood that you will be successful is MEDIUM (50%).

DECISION B. With both the attractiveness and likelihood information presented above in mind, indicate the level of effort you would exert to get this job.

0	1	2	3	4	5	6	7	8	9	10

Zero effort
to get it
                                                                                    Great effort
                                                                                    to get it

JOB # 19

In this job, the likelihood that a major portion of your duties will involve

—establishing and maintaining friendly relationships with others is... VERY LOW (5%)

—influencing the activities or thoughts of a number of individuals is .... VERY HIGH (95%)

—accomplishing difficult (but feasible) goals and later receiving detailed information about your personal performance is .... VERY LOW (5%)

DECISION A. With the factors and associated likelihood levels shown above in mind, indicate the attractiveness of this job to you.

−5   −4   −3   −2   −1   0   +1   +2   +3   +4   +5
Very   Very
Unattractive   Attractive

FURTHER INFORMATION ABOUT JOB #19 If you exert a great deal of effort to get this job, the likelihood that you will be successful is VERY HIGH (95%).

DECISION B. With both the attractiveness and likelihood information presented above in mind, indicate the level of effort you would exert to get this job.

0   1   2   3   4   5   6   7   8   9   10
Zero effort   Great effort
to get it   to get it

JOB # 20

In this job, the likelihood that a major portion of your duties will involve

—establishing and maintaining friendly relationships with others is... VERY HIGH (95%)

—influencing the activities or thoughts of a number of individuals is .... VERY HIGH (95%)

—accomplishing difficult (but feasible) goals and later receiving detailed information about your personal performance is .... VERY HIGH (95%)

DECISION A. With the factors and associated likelihood levels shown above in mind, indicate the attractiveness of this job to you.

−5   −4   −3   −2   −1   0   +1   +2   +3   +4   +5
Very   Very
Unattractive   Attractive

FURTHER INFORMATION ABOUT JOB #20 If you exert a great deal of effort to get this job, the likelihood that you will be successful is VERY LOW (5%).

DECISION B. With both the attractiveness and likelihood information presented above in mind, indicate the level of effort you would exert to get this job.

0   1   2   3   4   5   6   7   8   9   10
Zero effort   Great effort
to get it   to get it

© M. J. Stahl and A. M. Harrell, 1981

JOB # 21

*In this job, the likelihood that a major portion of your duties
will involve*

—*establishing and maintaining friendly relationships
with others is*..

VERY
HIGH (95%)

—*influencing the activities or thoughts of a number
of individuals is* ....

VERY
LOW (5%)

—*accomplishing difficult (but feasible) goals and
later receiving detailed information about your
personal performance is* ....

VERY
HIGH (95%)

DECISION A. With the factors and associated likelihood levels shown above
in mind, indicate the attractiveness of this job to you.

| −5 | −4 | −3 | −2 | −1 | 0 | +1 | +2 | +3 | +4 | +5 |

Very
Unattractive

Very
Attractive

*FURTHER INFORMATION ABOUT JOB #21 If you exert a great deal of effort to
get this job, the likelihood that you will be successful is VERY HIGH (95%).*
DECISION B. With both the attractiveness and likelihood information presented
above in mind, indicate the level of effort you would exert to get this job.

| 0 | 1 | 2 | 3 | 4 | 5 | 6 | 7 | 8 | 9 | 10 |

Zero effort
to get it

Great effort
to get it

JOB # 22

*In this job, the likelihood that a major portion of your duties
will involve*

—*establishing and maintaining friendly relationships
with others is*..

VERY
HIGH (95%)

—*influencing the activities or thoughts of a number
of individuals is* ....

VERY
HIGH (95%)

—*accomplishing difficult (but feasible) goals and
later receiving detailed information about your
personal performance is* ....

VERY
LOW (5%)

DECISION A. With the factors and associated likelihood levels shown above
in mind, indicate the attractiveness of this job to you.

| −5 | −4 | −3 | −2 | −1 | 0 | +1 | +2 | +3 | +4 | +5 |

Very
Unattractive

Very
Attractive

*FURTHER INFORMATION ABOUT JOB #22 If you exert a great deal of effort to
get this job, the likelihood that you will be successful is VERY LOW (5%).*
DECISION B. With both the attractiveness and likelihood information presented
above in mind, indicate the level of effort you would exert to get this job.

| 0 | 1 | 2 | 3 | 4 | 5 | 6 | 7 | 8 | 9 | 10 |

Zero effort
to get it

Great effort
to get it

JOB # 23

In this job, the likelihood that a major portion of your duties will involve

—*establishing and maintaining friendly relationships with others is*... VERY LOW (5%)

—*influencing the activities or thoughts of a number of individuals is* .... VERY LOW (5%)

—*accomplishing difficult (but feasible) goals and later receiving detailed information about your personal performance is* .... VERY HIGH (95%)

DECISION A. With the factors and associated likelihood levels shown above in mind, indicate the attractiveness of this job to you.

| −5 | −4 | −3 | −2 | −1 | 0 | +1 | +2 | +3 | +4 | +5 |

Very
Unattractive

Very
Attractive

FURTHER INFORMATION ABOUT JOB #23 If you exert a great deal of effort to get this job, the likelihood that you will be successful is VERY LOW (5%).

DECISION B. With both the attractiveness and likelihood information presented above in mind, indicate the level of effort you would exert to get this job.

| 0 | 1 | 2 | 3 | 4 | 5 | 6 | 7 | 8 | 9 | 10 |

Zero effort
to get it

Great effort
to get it

JOB # 24

In this job, the likelihood that a major portion of your duties will involve

—*establishing and maintaining friendly relationships with others is*... VERY LOW (5%)

—*influencing the activities or thoughts of a number of individuals is* .... VERY HIGH (95%)

—*accomplishing difficult (but feasible) goals and later receiving detailed information about your personal performance is* .... VERY LOW (5%)

DECISION A. With the factors and associated likelihood levels shown above in mind, indicate the attractiveness of this job to you.

| −5 | −4 | −3 | −2 | −1 | 0 | +1 | +2 | +3 | +4 | +5 |

Very
Unattractive

Very
Attractive

FURTHER INFORMATION ABOUT JOB #24 If you exert a great deal of effort to get this job, the likelihood that you will be successful is MEDIUM (50%).

DECISION B. With both the attractiveness and likelihood information presented above in mind, indicate the level of effort you would exert to get this job.

| 0 | 1 | 2 | 3 | 4 | 5 | 6 | 7 | 8 | 9 | 10 |

Zero effort
to get it

Great effort
to get it

© M. J. Stahl and A. M. Harrell, 1981

JOB # 25

In this job, the likelihood that a major portion of your duties will involve

—*establishing and maintaining friendly relationships with others is*... VERY LOW (5%)

—*influencing the activities or thoughts of a number of individuals is* .... VERY LOW (5%)

—*accomplishing difficult (but feasible) goals and later receiving detailed information about your personal performance is* .... VERY LOW (5%)

DECISION A. With the factors and associated likelihood levels shown above in mind, indicate the attractiveness of this job to you.

−5	−4	−3	−2	−1	0	+1	+2	+3	+4	+5

Very
Unattractive

Very
Attractive

FURTHER INFORMATION ABOUT JOB #25 If you exert a great deal of effort to get this job, the likelihood that you will be successful is VERY LOW (5%).

DECISION B. With both the attractiveness and likelihood information presented above in mind, indicate the level of effort you would exert to get this job.

0	1	2	3	4	5	6	7	8	9	10

Zero effort
to get it

Great effort
to get it

JOB # 26

In this job, the likelihood that a major portion of your duties will involve

—*establishing and maintaining friendly relationships with others is*... VERY HIGH (95%)

—*influencing the activities or thoughts of a number of individuals is* .... VERY LOW (5%)

—*accomplishing difficult (but feasible) goals and later receiving detailed information about your personal performance is* .... VERY LOW (5%)

DECISION A. With the factors and associated likelihood levels shown above in mind, indicate the attractiveness of this job to you.

−5	−4	−3	−2	−1	0	+1	+2	+3	+4	+5

Very
Unattractive

Very
Attractive

FURTHER INFORMATION ABOUT JOB #26 If you exert a great deal of effort to get this job, the likelihood that you will be successful is VERY HIGH (95%).

DECISION B. With both the attractiveness and likelihood information presented above in mind, indicate the level of effort you would exert to get this job.

0	1	2	3	4	5	6	7	8	9	10

Zero effort
to get it

Great effort
to get it

JOB # 27

In this job, the likelihood that a major portion of your duties will involve

—establishing and maintaining friendly relationships with others is.. **VERY HIGH** (95%)

—influencing the activities or thoughts of a number of individuals is .... **VERY HIGH** (95%)

—accomplishing difficult (but feasible) goals and later receiving detailed information about your personal performance is .... **VERY HIGH** (95%)

DECISION A. With the factors and associated likelihood levels shown above in mind, indicate the attractiveness of this job to you.

−5 −4 −3 −2 −1 0 +1 +2 +3 +4 +5
Very   Very
Unattractive   Attractive

FURTHER INFORMATION ABOUT JOB #27 If you exert a great deal of effort to get this job, the likelihood that you will be successful is MEDIUM (50%).

DECISION B. With both the attractiveness and likelihood information presented above in mind, indicate the level of effort you would exert to get this job.

0 1 2 3 4 5 6 7 8 9 10
Zero effort   Great effort
to get it   to get it

JOB # 28

In this job, the likelihood that a major portion of your duties will involve

—establishing and maintaining friendly relationships with others is.. **VERY HIGH** (95%)

—influencing the activities or thoughts of a number of individuals is .... **VERY LOW** (5%)

—accomplishing difficult (but feasible) goals and later receiving detailed information about your personal performance is .... **VERY HIGH** (95%)

DECISION A. With the factors and associated likelihood levels shown above in mind, indicate the attractiveness of this job to you.

−5 −4 −3 −2 −1 0 +1 +2 +3 +4 +5
Very   Very
Unattractive   Attractive

FURTHER INFORMATION ABOUT JOB #28 If you exert a great deal of effort to get this job, the likelihood that you will be successful is MEDIUM (50%).

DECISION B. With both the attractiveness and likelihood information presented above in mind, indicate the level of effort you would exert to get this job.

0 1 2 3 4 5 6 7 8 9 10
Zero effort   Great effort
to get it   to get it

© M. J. Stahl and A. M. Harrell, 1981

JOB # 29

In this job, the likelihood that a major portion of your duties will involve

—establishing and maintaining friendly relationships with others is... VERY LOW (5%)

—influencing the activities or thoughts of a number of individuals is .... VERY HIGH (95%)

—accomplishing difficult (but feasible) goals and later receiving detailed information about your personal performance is .... VERY HIGH (95%)

DECISION A. With the factors and associated likelihood levels shown above in mind, indicate the attractiveness of this job to you.

| −5 | −4 | −3 | −2 | −1 | 0 | +1 | +2 | +3 | +4 | +5 |

Very
Unattractive   Very
                                                                             Attractive

FURTHER INFORMATION ABOUT JOB #29 If you exert a great deal of effort to get this job, the likelihood that you will be successful is VERY HIGH (95%).

DECISION B. With both the attractiveness and likelihood information presented above in mind, indicate the level of effort you would exert to get this job.

| 0 | 1 | 2 | 3 | 4 | 5 | 6 | 7 | 8 | 9 | 10 |

Zero effort
to get it   Great effort
                                                                             to get it

JOB # 30

In this job, the likelihood that a major portion of your duties will involve

—establishing and maintaining friendly relationships with others is... VERY HIGH (95%)

—influencing the activities or thoughts of a number of individuals is .... VERY HIGH (95%)

—accomplishing difficult (but feasible) goals and later receiving detailed information about your personal performance is .... VERY LOW (5%)

DECISION A. With the factors and associated likelihood levels shown above in mind, indicate the attractiveness of this job to you.

| −5 | −4 | −3 | −2 | −1 | 0 | +1 | +2 | +3 | +4 | +5 |

Very
Unattractive   Very
                                                                             Attractive

FURTHER INFORMATION ABOUT JOB #30 If you exert a great deal of effort to get this job, the likelihood that you will be successful is MEDIUM (50%).

DECISION B. With both the attractiveness and likelihood information presented above in mind, indicate the level of effort you would exert to get this job.

| 0 | 1 | 2 | 3 | 4 | 5 | 6 | 7 | 8 | 9 | 10 |

Zero effort
to get it   Great effort
                                                                             to get it

Bibliography

Adams, A. J., and Stone, T. H. (1977) Satisfaction for achievement in work and leisure time activities. *Journal of Vocational Behavior, 11,* 174-181.

American Psychological Association, Division of Industrial-Organizational Psychology. (1980) *Principles for the Validation and Use of Personnel Selection Procedures.* (Second Edition) Berkeley, CA: APA.

Arnold, H. J. (1981) A test of the multiplicative hypothesis of expectancy-valence theories of work motivation. *Academy of Management Journal, 24,* 128-141.

Arnold, H. J., and Feldman, D. C. (1981) Social desirability response bias in self-report choice situations. *Academy of Management Journal, 24,* 377-385.

Ashton, R. (1974) Cue utilization and expert judgments: A comparison of independent auditors with other judges. *Journal of Applied Psychology, 59,* 437-444.

Atkinson, J. W. (1977) Personality variables in social behavior. In T. Blass (Ed.), *Motivation for Achievement,* 25-108. Hillsdale, NJ: Erlbaum Associates.

Bedeian, A. G., and Hyder, J. L. (1977) Sex-role attitude as a moderator in the relationship between locus of control and n Achievement. *Psychological Reports, 41,* 1172-1174.

Benel, R. A. (1976) Note on the relationship between n Ach and uric acid. *Psychological Reports, 39,* 524-526.

Borysenko, J., and Borysenko, M. (1983) On psychoneuroimmunology: How the mind influences health and disease, and how to make the influence beneficial. *Executive Health, 19(10),* 1-7.

Boyatzis, R. E. (1973) Affiliation motivation. In D. C. McClelland and R. Steele (Eds.), *Human Motivation: A Book of Readings,* 253-257. New York: General Learning Press.

Brief, A. P., Aldag, R. J., and Chacko, T. I. (1977) The Miner Sentence Completion Scale: An appraisal. *Academy of Management Journal, 20,* 635-643.

Brief, A. P., Aldag, R. J., and Russell, C. J. (1979) An analysis of power in a work setting. *The Journal of Social Psychology, 109*, 289-295.

Brown, R. R. (1972) A comparison of judgmental policy equations obtained from human judges under natural and contrived conditions. *Mathematical Biosciences, 15*, 205-230.

Brunswik, E. (1952) *The Conceptual Framework of Psychology*. Chicago: University of Chicago Press.

Butler, R. P., Lardent, C. L., and Miner, J. B. (1983) A motivational basis for turnover in military officer education and training. *Journal of Applied Psychology, 68*, 496-506.

Campbell, J. P., Dunnette, M. D., Lawler, E. E., and Weick, K. E. (1970) *Managerial Behavior, Performance and Effectiveness.* New York: McGraw-Hill.

Cascio, W. (1982) *Applied Psychology in Personal Management.* (Second Edition) Reston, VA: Reston Publishing.

Clarke, David E. (1972) Measures of achievement and affiliation motivation. *Review of Educational Research, 43*, 41-51.

Cornelius, E. T., III. (1983) The use of projective techniques in personnel selection. In K. M. Rowland and G. D. Ferris (Eds.), *Research in Personnel and Human Resources Management.* New York: JAI Press.

Cornelius, E. T., III, and Lane, F. B. (1984) The power motive and managerial success in a professionally oriented service industry organization. *Journal of Applied Psychology, 69*, 32-39.

Cronbach, L. J., and Meehl, P. E. (1955) Construct validity in psychological tests. *Psychological Bulletin, 52*, 281-301.

Crowne, D. P., and Marlowe, D. (1960) A new scale of social desirability independent of psychopathology. *Journal of Counseling Psychology, 24*, 349-354.

Cummin, P. (1967) TAT correlates of executive performance. *Journal of Applied Psychology, 51*, 78-81.

Dalton, D. R., and Todor, W. C. (1979) Manifest needs of stewards: Propensity to file a grievance. *Journal of Applied Psychology, 64*, 654-659.

Darlington, R. B. (1968) Multiple regression in psychological research and practice. *Psychological Bulletin, 69*, 161-182.

Decharms, R. (1957) Affiliation motivation and productivity in small groups. *Journal of Abnormal and Social Psychology, 55*, 222-226.

Depner, C. E., and Veroff, J. (1979) Varieties of achievement motivation. *The Journal of Social Psychology, 107*, 283-284.

Donley, R. E., and Winter, D. G. (1970) Measuring the motives of public officials at a distance: An explanatory study of American presidents. *Behavioral Science, 15*, 227-236.

Durand, D. E. (1975a) Effect of drinking on the power and affiliation needs of middle aged females. *Journal of Clinical Psychology, 31*, 549-553.

——. (1975b) Relation of achievement and power motives to performance among black businessmen. *Psychological Reports, 37*, 11-14.

Einhorn, H. J., and Hogarth, R. M. (1981) Behavioral decision theory: Process of judgment and choice. *Annual Review of Psychology, 32*, 53-88.

Entwisle, D. R. (1972) To dispel fantasies about fantasy-based measures of achievement motivation. *Psychological Bulletin, 77*, 377-391.

Fineman, S. (1977) The achievement motive construct and its measurement: Where are we now? *British Journal of Psychology, 68*, 1-22.

Friedman, M., Rosenmann, R. H., and Carroll, V. (1957) Changes in the serum cholesterol and blood clotting time of men subject to cyclic variation of occupational stress. *Circulation, 17*, 852-861.

Garrison, J. P., and Pate, L. E. (1977) Toward development and measurement of the interpersonal power construct. *Journal of Psychology, 97*, 95-106.

Ghiselli, E. E. (1971) *Explorations in Managerial Talent.* Pacific Palisades, CA: Goodyear.

Glass, G. V. (1976) Primary, secondary and meta-analysis of research. *Educational Researcher, 10*, 3-8.

Glass, G. V., McGaw, B., and Smith, M. L. (1981) *Meta-analysis in Social Research.* Beverly Hills, CA: Sage Publications.

Goldberg, L. R. (1968) Simple models or simple processes? Some research on clinical judgments. *American Psychologist, 23*, 483-496.

Goodman, P. S., Rose, J. H., and Furcon, J. E. (1970) Comparison of motivational antecedents of the work performance of scientists and engineers. *Journal of Applied Psychology, 14*, 491-495.

Guilford, J. P. (1954) *Psychometric Methods.* (Second Edition) New York: McGraw-Hill.

Hamburg, David A., Elliott, Glen R., and Parron, Delores L. (1982) *Health and Behavior: Frontiers of Research in the Biobehavioral Sciences.* Washington, D.C.: National Academy Press.

Hamby, R. (1978) Effect of power on moral judgment. *Psychological Reports, 42*, 387-394.

Hammond, K. R., Rohrbaugh, J., Mumpower, J., and Adelman, A. (1977) Social judgment theory: Applications in policy formation. In M. F. Kaplan and S. Schwartz (Eds.), *Human Judgment and Decision Process in Applied Settings.* New York: Academic Press.

Hampton, Summer, and Webber. (1982) *Organizational Behavior and the Practice of Management.* (Fourth Edition) Glenview IL: Scott Foresman.

Harrell, A. M., and Stahl, M. J. (1981) A behavioral decision theory approach for measuring McClelland's trichotomy of needs. *Journal of Applied Psychology, 66*, 242-247.

Helmreich, R., Beane, W., Lucker, W., and Spence, J. (1978) Achievement motivation and scientific attainment. *Personality and Social Psychology Bulletin, 4*, 222-226.

Hendrix, W. H., and Stahl, M. J. (1984) Association of need for power with cortisol, cholesterol and blood pressure. *Proceedings, 1984 Southern Management Association Meeting,* 1-3. New Orleans: S.M.A.

Herzberg, F., Mausner, B., and Synderman, B. (1959) *The Motivation to Work.* New York: Wiley.

Hines, G. H. (1973) Achievement motivation, occupation, and labor turnover in New Zealand. *Journal of Applied Psychology, 58 (3)*, 313-317.

Hoffman, B. (1980) *Power Quotients: Relationship to Bodysize.* York, PA: York Barbell Co.

Hoffman, P. J. (1960) The paramorphic representation of clinical judgment. *Psychological Bulletin, 57,* 116-132.

Hom, P. W., Katerberg, R., and Hulin, C. L. (1979) Comparative examination of three approaches to the prediction of turnover. *Journal of Applied Psychology, 64,* 280-290.

Kanungo, R. N. (1980) Affiliation and autonomy under stress. *Psychological Reports, 46,* 13-40.

Kaplan, M. F., and Schwartz, S. (Eds.) (1975) *Human Judgment and Decision Process.* New York: Academic Press.

Kroll, W., and Petersen, K. H. (1965) Personality factor profiles of collegiate football teams. *Research Quarterly, 36,* 433-439.

Libby, R. (1975) Accounting ratios and the prediction of failure: Some behavioral evidence. *Journal of Accounting Research, 13,* 150-161.

——. (1981) *Accounting and Human Information Processing: Theory and Applications.* Englewood Cliffs, NJ: Prentice-Hall.

Lord, F. M. (1971) On the statistical treatment of football numbers. In J. A. Steger (Ed.), *Readings in Statistics for the Behavioral Scientist.* New York: Holt, Rinehart & Winston.

Luthans, F. (1985) *Organizational Behavior.* New York: McGraw-Hill.

Manolis, G. G. (1955) Relation of charging time to blocking performance in football. *Research Quarterly, 26,* 170-178.

Maslach, C., and Jackson, S. E. (1981) The measurement of experimental burnout. *Journal of Occupational Behavior, 2,* 99-113.

Maslow, A. H. (1943) A theory of human motivation. *Psychological Review, 50,* 370-396.

Matter, D. E. (1977) Achievement motivation in high school graduates (1907-1967) and occupational correlates. *Psychological Reports, 41,* 1271-1274.

McClelland, D. C. (1954) The recruitment of scientific psychologists. *American Psychologist, 9*, 811-813.

———. (1956) The calculated risk: An aspect of creative scientific performance. In D. W. Taylor (Ed.), *Research Conference on the Identification of Creative Scientific Talent*. Salt Lake City: University of Utah Press.

———. (1961) *The Achieving Society*. New York: Van Nostrand.

———. (1962a) Business drives and national achievement. *Harvard Business Review, 42*, 103-105.

———. (1962b) On the psychodynamics of creative physical scientists. In H. E. Gauber, G. Terrell, and M. Mertheimer (Eds.), *Contemporary Approaches to Creative Thinking*. New York: Atherton Press.

———. (1965a) N Achievement and entrepreneurship: A longitudinal study. *Journal of Personality and Social Psychology, 1*, 389-392.

———. (1965b) Achievement motivation can be developed. *Harvard Business Review, 43*, 6-24.

———. (1970) The two faces of power. *Journal of International Affairs, 24*, 29-47.

———. (1975a) Love and power: The psychological signals of war. *Psychology Today, 8*, 44-48.

———. (1975b) *Power: The Inner Experience*. New York: Irvington Publishers.

———. (1978) Entrepreneurship and management in the years ahead. In C. A. Baramelet and M. H. Mescon (Eds.), *The Individual and the Future of the Organization*. Atlanta: Georgia State College of Business Administration.

———. (1979a) Inhibited power motivation and high blood pressure in men. *Journal of Abnormal Psychology, 88*, 182-190.

———. (1979b) That urge to achieve. In D. A. Kolb, I. M. Rubin, and J. M. McIntyre (Eds.), *Organizational Psychology: A Book of Readings*. Englewood Cliffs, NJ: Prentice-Hall.

———. (1981) Is personality consistent? In A. I. Rubin, J. Aranoff, A. M. Barclay, and R. A. Zucker (Eds.), *Further Exploration in Personality*. New York: Wiley.

McClelland, D. C., Alexander, C., and Marks, E. (1982) The need for power, stress, immune function, and illness among male prisoners. *Journal of Abnormal Psychology, 91*, 61-70.

McClelland, D. C., Atkinson, J., Clark, R., and Lowell, E. (1976) *The Achievement Motive.* New York: Irvington Publishers.

McClelland, D. C., and Boyatzis, R. E. (1982) Leadership motive pattern and longterm success in management. *Journal of Applied Psychology, 67*, 737-743.

McClelland, D. C., and Burnham, D. H. (1976) Power is the great motivator. *Harvard Business Review, 54*, 100-110.

McClelland, D. C., Davis, W. N., Kalin, R., and Wonne, F. (1972) *The Drinking Man*, 332-336. New York: The Free Press.

McClelland, D. C., Floor, E., Davidson, R. J., and Saron, C. (1980) Stressed power motivation, sympathetic activation, immune function, and illness. *Journal of Human Stress, 6 (2)*, 11-19.

McClelland, D. C., and Jemmott, J. B. (1980) Power motivation, stress and physical illness. *Journal of Human Stress, 6 (4)*, 6-15.

McClelland, D. C., and Teague, G. (1975) Predicting risk preferences among power related tasks. *Journal of Personality, 43*, 226-285.

McClelland, D. C., and Watson, R. I., Jr. (1973) Power motivation and risk taking behavior. *Journal of Personality, 41*, 121-139.

McClelland, D. C., and Winter, D. (1969). *Motivating Economic Achievement.* New York: The Free Press.

McDavid, R. F. (1977) Predicting potential in football players. *Research Quarterly, 48*, 99-104.

Melikian, L., Girisberg, A., Cuceloglu, D., and Lynn, R. (1971) Achievement motivation in Afghanistan, Brazil, Saudi Arabia, and Turkey. *The Journal of Social Psychology, 83*, 183-184.

Miles, W. R. (1931) Studies in physical exertion II: Individual and group reaction time in football charging. *Research Quarterly, 2*, 5-13.

Miner, J. B. (1960) The effect of a course in psychology on the attitudes of research and development supervisors. *Journal of Applied Psychology, 44,* 224-232.

——. (1964) *Scoring Guide for the Miner Sentence Completion Scale.* Atlanta: Organizational Measurement Systems Press.

——. (1977a) Implications of managerial talent projections for management education. *Academy of Management Review, 2,* 412-420.

——. (1977b) *Scoring Guide for the Miner Sentence Completion Scale: 1977 Supplement.* Atlanta: Organizational Measurement Systems Press.

——. (1978a) The Miner Sentence Completion Scale: A reappraisal. *Academy of Management Journal, 21,* 283-294.

——. (1978b) Twenty years of research on role-motivation theory of managerial effectiveness. *Personnel Psychology, 31,* 739-760.

Miner, J. B., and Crane, D. P. (1981) Motivation to manage and the manifestation of a managerial orientation in career planning. *Academy of Management Journal, 24,* 626-633.

Miner, J. B., and Smith, N. R. (1982) Decline and stabilization of managerial motivation over a 20-year period. *Journal of Applied Psychology, 67,* 297-305.

Miron, D., and McClelland, D. C. (1979) The impact of achievement motivation training on small businesses. *California Management Review, 21,* 13-28.

Mitchell, T. R., and Beach, L. R. (1977) Expectancy theory, decision theory, and occupational preference and choice. In M. F. Kaplan and S. Schwartz (Eds.), *Human Judgment and Decision Process in Applied Settings.* New York: Academic Press.

Mora, M. E. F. (1984) Motivacion de Logro, Afiliacion y Poder de Estudiantes de Ingeniera Electronica y Administracion de Empresas de la Usma. M.S. thesis, University of Panama.

Neiner, A. G., and Owens, W. A. (1985) Using biodata to predict job choice among college graduates. *Journal of Applied Psychology, 70,* 127-136.

Nunnally, J. C. (1967) *Psychometric Theory.* New York: McGraw-Hill.

Owens, W. A., and Shoenfeldt, L. F. (1979) Toward a classification of persons. *Journal of Applied Psychology, 65*, 569-607.

Query, J. M. N. (1975) Independence training, need achievement and need affiliation between white and Indian children. *International Journal of Psychology, 10*, 255-268.

Quick, J. C., and Quick, J. D. (1984) *Organizational Stress and Preventive Management.* New York: McGraw-Hill.

Ritchie, R. J., and Moses, J. L. (1983) Assessment center correlates of women's advancement into middle management: A seven-year longitudinal analysis. *Journal of Applied Psychology, 68*, 227-231.

Rubenfeld, S. A., and Crino, M. D. (1981) The uniform guidelines: A personnel decision-making perspective. *Employee Relations Law Journal, 7*, 105-121.

Rushall, B. S. (1972) Three studies relating personality variables to football performance. *Journal of Sports Psychology, 3*, 12-24.

Russek, H. I. (1965) Stress, tobacco, and coronary disease in North American professional groups. *Journal of the American Medical Association, 192*, 189-194.

Schachter, S. (1959) *The Psychology of Affiliation.* Stanford, CA: Stanford University Press.

Schnieder, F. W., and Green, J. E. (1977) Need for affiliation and sex as moderators of the relationship between need for achievement and academic performance. *Journal of School Psychology, 15*, 269-277.

Singh, S. (1978) Achievement motivation and entrepreneurial success: A follow up study. *Journal of Research in Personality, 19*, 500-503.

———. (1979) Relationship among projective and direct verbal measures of achievement motivation. *Journal of Personality Assessment, 43*, 45-49.

Slovic, P. (1969) Analyzing the expert judge: A descriptive study of a stockbroker's decision process. *Journal of Applied Psychology, 55*, 225-263.

Slovic, P., Fischhoff, B., and Lichtenstein, S. (1977) Behavioral decision theory. *Annual Review of Psychology, 28*, 1-39.

Slovic, P., and Lichtenstein, S. (1971) Comparison of Bayesian and regression approaches to the study of information processing judgment. *Organizational Behavior and Human Performance, 6*, 649-744.

Stahl, M. J. (1983) Achievement, power and managerial motivation: Selecting managerial talent with the Job Choice Exercise. *Personnel Psychology, 36*, 775-789.

——. (1986) Selecting and training managerial talent among scientists and engineers: Power motivates. *Research Management*, in press.

Stahl, M. J., Christoph, R. T., and Harrell, A. M. (1982) Identifying high and low managerial motivation: Applying McClelland's theory and the Job Choice Exercise. *Proceedings, Southern Management Association Meeting*, 358-360. New Orleans: S.M.A.

Stahl, M. J., Grigsby, D., and Gulati, A. (1985) Comparing the Job Choice Exercise and the multiple choice version of the Miner Sentence Completion Scale. *Journal of Applied Psychology, 70*, 228-232.

Stahl, M. J., and Harrell, A. M. (1979) Behavioral decision theory, need for achievement and academic performance. *Proceedings, Western AIDS Meeting*, 162-164. Reno: Western AIDS.

——. (1981) Modeling effort decisions with behavioral decision theory: Toward an individual differences version of expectancy theory. *Organizational Behavior and Human Performance, 27*, 303-325.

——. (1982) Evolution and validation of a behavioral decision theory measurement approach to achievement, power, and affiliation. *Journal of Applied Psychology, 67*, 744-751.

——. (1983) Using decision modeling to measure second level valences in expectancy theory. *Organizational Behavior and Human Performance, 32*, 23-24.

Stahl, M. J., and Koser, M. C. (1978) Weighted productivity in R&D: Some associated individual and orgnizational variables. *IEEE Transactions of Engineering Management, EM-25*, 20-24.

Steers, R. M. (1981) *Introduction to Organizational Behavior*. Santa Monica, CA: Goodyear Publishing.

Steers, R. M., and Braunstein, D. M. (1976) A behaviorally-based measure of manifest needs in work settings. *Journal of Vocational Behavior, 9*, 251-266.

Steers, R. M., and Spencer, D. G. (1977) The role of achievement motivation in job design. *Journal of Personality, 62*, 472-479.

Steger, J. A. (1978) How RPI helps locate talent. *Business Week*, September 18, 129-131.

Steger, J. A., Kelly, W. B., Chouiniere, B., and Goldenbaum, A. (1975) A forced choice version of the MSCS and how it discriminates campus leaders and non-leaders. *Academy of Management Journal, 18*, 453-460.

Steger, J. A., Manners, G., Bernstein, A. J., and May, R. (1975) The three dimensions of the R&D managers job. *Research Management, 18*, 32-37.

Szilagyi, A. D., and Wallace, M. J. (1983) *Organizational Behavior and Performance* (Third Edition) Glenview, IL: Scott, Foresman.

Teevan, R. C., and Yalof, J. (1980) Need for achievement in "starting" and in "non-starting" varsity athletes. *Perceptual and Motor Skills, 50*, 402.

Varga, K. (1975) N achievement, n power and effectiveness of research development. *Human Relations, 28*, 571-590.

Veroff, J. (1969) Social comparison and the development of achievement motivation. In C. P. Smith (Ed.), *Achievement-Related Motives in Children.* New York: Russell Sage.

———. (1982) Assertive motivations: Achievement versus power. In A. J. Stewart (Ed.), *Motivation and Society: A Volume in Honor of David C. McClelland.* San Francisco: Jossey-Bass.

Veroff, J., Depner, C., Kulka, R., and Douvan, E. (1980) Comparison of American motives: 1957 vs. 1976. *Journal of Personality and Social Psychology, 39*, 1249-1262.

Veroff, J., Feld, S., and Gurin, G. (1962) Achievement motivation and religious background. *American Sociological Review, 27*, 205-217.

Veroff, J., McClelland, L., and Ruhland, D. (1975) Varieties of achievement motivation. In M. Medrick, S. Tangri, and L. Hoffman (Eds.), *Women and Achievement.* Washington, D.C.: Hemisphere.

Vroom, V. H. (1964) *Work and Motivation.* New York: Wiley.

Wainer, H. A., and Rubin, I. M. (1969) Motivation of research and development entrepreneurs: Determinants of company success. *Journal of Applied Psychology, 53,* 178-184.

Ward, J. H., Jr. (1962) Comments on the paramorphic representation of clinical judgment. *Psychological Bulletin, 59,* 74-76.

Weiner, H. (1970) Psychosomatic research in essential hypertension: Retrospect and prospect. In M. Koster, H. Musaph, and P. Visser (Eds.), *Psychosomatics in Essential Hypertension,* 58-116. Basel: S. Karger.

Werner, A. W., and E. Gottheil. (1955) Personality and participation in college athletes. *Research Quarterly, 24,* 126-131.

Winter, D. G. (1973) *The Power Motive.* New York: The Free Press.

Winter, D. G., and Stewart, A. J. (1977) Power motive reliability as a function of retest instructions. *Journal of Consulting and Clinical Psychology, 45,* 436-444.

Yamauch, H., and Doi, K. (1977) Factorial study of achievement related motives. *Psychological Reports, 41,* 795-801.

Zedeck, S. (1977) An information processing model approach to the study of motivation. *Organizational Behavior and Human Performance, 18,* 47-77.

Index

About the Author

MICHAEL J. STAHL received his Ph.D. in Management in 1975 from Rensselaer Polytechnic Institute. Dr. Stahl conducted research into new technologies for measuring motivation employing behavioral decision theory in the late 1970s while teaching graduate-level courses at the Air Force Institute of Technology. Dr. Stahl has continued that research since moving to Clemson University in 1980. He is currently Professor and Head of the Department of Management at Clemson.

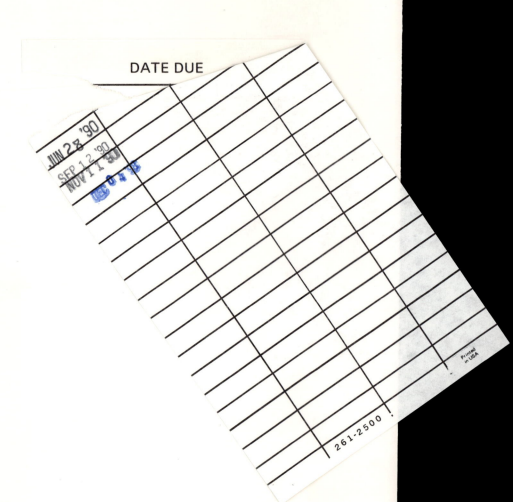